EUROPEAN POLITICAL, ECONOMIC, AND SECURITY ISSUES

A HISTORY OF VOTING RIGHTS FOR PARLIAMENTARY ELECTIONS IN THE UNITED KINGDOM

EUROPEAN POLITICAL, ECONOMIC, AND SECURITY ISSUES

Additional books in this series can be found on Nova's website
under the Series tab.

Additional e-books in this series can be found on Nova's website
under the e-book tab.

EUROPEAN POLITICAL, ECONOMIC, AND SECURITY ISSUES

A HISTORY OF VOTING RIGHTS FOR PARLIAMENTARY ELECTIONS IN THE UNITED KINGDOM

NICOLE P. SPRINGER
EDITOR

nova
publishers
New York

NOTICE TO THE READER

Library of Congress Cataloging-in-Publication Data

ISBN: 978-1-62948-870-7

Published by Nova Science Publishers, Inc. † *New York*

CONTENTS

PREFACE

This book gives a history of the Parliamentary franchise and shows the incremental stages which led to universal suffrage across the UK by drawing on several of the recognised sources which have dealt with the subject and by referring to the key legislation. It also provides background to the provisions relating to overseas voters in the Representation of the People Act 1985 which was subsequently amended by the Representation of the People Act 1989 and the Political Parties, Elections and Referendums Act 2000. There has been considerable concern about the under-registration of the Armed Forces, especially those serving overseas, and the difficulties they face in participating in the electoral process generally. This book continues with giving details of recent changes to legislation, including the provisions of the Electoral Administration Act 2006, and information about measures taken to increase the electoral registration of service personnel. The final chapter of the book briefly draws together library material on the issue of prisoners' voting rights.

Chapter 1 - The right to vote in Parliamentary elections had been virtually unchanged from medieval times until the Great Reform Act of 1832. The qualifications to vote differed in the four nations of the United Kingdom and within each country the right to vote was different depending where you lived. County voters had different qualifications to those in the boroughs and each borough had its own requirements on eligibility. Not every borough had the right to return an MP.

Registration of Parliamentary electors was not required (except in the Irish counties following the inclusion of Irish seats in the post-Union Westminster Parliament). Voters had to prove their right to vote before casting a public ballot. Secret ballots were not introduced until 1872.

Opportunities to cast votes in Parliamentary elections were further limited by the absence of contested elections in many instances. Uncontested elections were common and in some seats an election had not taken place for many years. Parliamentary seats were often considered as property and remained in the control of a family from one generation to the next. This persisted until the beginning of the twentieth century.

The reforms of the nineteenth century started with the Great Reform Act of 1832 although this legislation only dealt with the position in England and Wales. Scotland and Ireland had separate pieces of legislation. The distinctions between county and borough voting qualifications were retained. The county vote was extended to include new categories but was still inked to property value. New uniform borough voting qualifications were created although some of the ancient rights were retained.

Voter registration was required across the whole of the UK for the first time after 1832. A fee was charged for registration and a qualifying period of residence was required.

The Second Reform Act of 1867 again only affected England and Wales. Separate legislation was required for Scotland and Ireland. This reform increased the electorate in the borough electorates and included many working class men.

The Third Reform Act was the first UK-wide reform. It introduced a uniform Parliamentary franchise qualification across all parts of the UK and equalised the franchise between county and borough voters. This change benefited working class county voters the most and led to a 70% increase in those eligible to register to vote. Although this was a significant advance still only about one quarter of the adult population (those 21 years or over) could register to vote.

The *Representation of the People Act 1918* saw the most significant advance in the Parliamentary franchise. All previous voting qualifications were repealed and universal male suffrage based on residence, and not on property ownership, was established. Women over 30 years of age who qualified for a local government vote or, if they were married, their husband qualified for a local government vote, were able to register to vote in Parliamentary elections for the first time. The 1918 Act also introduced absent voting for the military for the first time. Following the 1918 Act 74% of the adult population could register to vote in Parliamentary elections.

Universal adult suffrage was first achieved in the United Kingdom in 1928. The *Representation of the People (Equal Franchise) Act 1928* gave men and women the right to vote in Parliamentary elections on an equal basis. The current voting age of 18 was established in 1969.

Since 1969 there have been two significant developments in voting at Parliamentary elections, allowing voting in general elections to overseas voters and extending the availability of absent voting by proxy or postal voting.

The Parliamentary franchise was extended to allow overseas voters to register to vote in the constituency in which they were last registered for up to five years after leaving. This time limit was extended to 20 years in 1989 but reduced to 15 years in 2002.

Absent voting was extended to anyone who was unable to vote in person in 1985 but voters had to provide electoral registration administrators with the reason that an absent vote was required. In 2001 voters no longer had to provide a reason and any voter could apply for an absent vote on demand.

Chapter 2 - British citizens living overseas are entitled to be registered to vote in UK Parliamentary elections for up to 15 years in the constituency they were registered in before leaving the UK. They are not entitled to vote in UK local elections or elections to the devolved assemblies.

There have been calls for the 15 year rule to be changed, most recently during the passage of the *Electoral Registration and Administration Act 2013* but the Government has indicated that it has no plans to alter the arrangements for overseas voters at the moment.

Harry Shindler, a British citizen who has lived in Italy since 1982, and who has therefore not been able to vote in UK Parliamentary elections since 1997, took his case to the European Court of Human Rights in 2009 and argued that no time limit should be imposed on the right of British citizens living overseas to vote in the UK. In its judgment on 7 May 2013, the European Court ruled that there had been no violation of Article 3 of Protocol No 1 (right to free elections) of the European Convention on Human Rights and determined that the UK had legitimately confined the parliamentary franchise to those citizens who had 'a close connection to the UK and who would therefore be most directly affected by its laws.'

This Note provides background to the provisions relating to overseas voters in the *Representation of the People Act 1985* which was subsequently amended by the *Representation of the People Act 1989* and the *Political Parties, Elections and Referendums Act 2000*. Information is also given about the procedure for registering to vote as an overseas elector and the means of voting, either by post or by proxy.

There are different arrangements for the armed forces and these are covered in Library Standard Note SN/PC/4276, *Armed forces voting*.

Chapter 3 - This is an edited, reformatted and augmented version of the House of Commons Library Standard Note SN04276. The paper contains Parliamentary information licensed under the Open Parliament Licence v1.0, dated July 12, 2011.

Chapter 4 – This is an edited, reformatted and augmented version of the House of Commons Library (United Kingdom) Standard Note SN06480. The paper contains Parliamentary information licensed under the Open Parliament Licence v1.0., dated October 16, 2013.

In: A History of Voting Rights …   ISBN: 978-1-62948-870-7
Editor: Nicole P. Springer   © 2014 Nova Science Publishers, Inc.

Chapter 1

THE HISTORY OF THE PARLIAMENTARY FRANCHISE[*]

Neil Johnston

This paper gives a history of the Parliamentary franchise and shows the incremental stages which led to universal suffrage across the UK by drawing on several of the recognised sources which have dealt with the subject and by referring to the key legislation.

It gives a summary of eligibility to vote in Parliamentary elections before the reforms of the nineteenth century and then gives the main changes introduced by the Reform Acts of 1832, 1867/8 and 1884. The paper also gives details of the main changes of the Representation of the People Acts which created universal male suffrage, the first female suffrage and then universal adult suffrage.

The paper also briefly summarises the main reasons for disqualification from eligibility to vote and also briefly describes the extension of the Parliamentary franchise to 18 year olds in 1969 and to overseas voters in 1985.

Neil Johnston

---

[*] This paper (Research Paper 13/14) was published by the House of Commons Library (United Kingdom) March 2013. The paper contains Parliamentary information licensed under the Open Parliament Licence v1.0.

SUMMARY

The right to vote in Parliamentary elections had been virtually unchanged from medieval times until the Great Reform Act of 1832. The qualifications to vote differed in the four nations of the United Kingdom and within each country the right to vote was different depending where you lived. County voters had different qualifications to those in the boroughs and each borough had its own requirements on eligibility. Not every borough had the right to return an MP.

Registration of Parliamentary electors was not required (except in the Irish counties following the inclusion of Irish seats in the post-Union Westminster Parliament). Voters had to prove their right to vote before casting a public ballot. Secret ballots were not introduced until 1872.

Opportunities to cast votes in Parliamentary elections were further limited by the absence of contested elections in many instances. Uncontested elections were common and in some seats an election had not taken place for many years. Parliamentary seats were often considered as property and remained in the control of a family from one generation to the next. This persisted until the beginning of the twentieth century.

The reforms of the nineteenth century started with the Great Reform Act of 1832 although this legislation only dealt with the position in England and Wales. Scotland and Ireland had separate pieces of legislation. The distinctions between county and borough voting qualifications were retained. The county vote was extended to include new categories but was still inked to property value. New uniform borough voting qualifications were created although some of the ancient rights were retained.

Voter registration was required across the whole of the UK for the first time after 1832. A fee was charged for registration and a qualifying period of residence was required.

The Second Reform Act of 1867 again only affected England and Wales. Separate legislation was required for Scotland and Ireland. This reform increased the electorate in the borough electorates and included many working class men.

The Third Reform Act was the first UK-wide reform. It introduced a uniform Parliamentary franchise qualification across all parts of the UK and equalised the franchise between county and borough voters. This change benefited working class county voters the most and led to a 70% increase in those eligible to register to vote. Although this was a significant advance still only about one quarter of the adult population (those 21 years or over) could register to vote.

The *Representation of the People Act 1918* saw the most significant advance in the Parliamentary franchise. All previous voting qualifications were repealed and universal male suffrage based on residence, and not on property ownership, was established. Women over 30 years of age who qualified for a local government vote or, if they were married, their husband qualified for a local government vote, were able to register to vote in Parliamentary elections for the first time. The 1918 Act also introduced absent voting for the military for the first time. Following the 1918 Act 74% of the adult population could register to vote in Parliamentary elections.

Universal adult suffrage was first achieved in the United Kingdom in 1928. The *Representation of the People (Equal Franchise) Act 1928* gave men and women the right to vote in Parliamentary elections on an equal basis. The current voting age of 18 was established in 1969.

Since 1969 there have been two significant developments in voting at Parliamentary elections, allowing voting in general elections to overseas voters and extending the availability of absent voting by proxy or postal voting.

The Parliamentary franchise was extended to allow overseas voters to register to vote in the constituency in which they were last registered for up to five years after leaving. This time limit was extended to 20 years in 1989 but reduced to 15 years in 2002.

Absent voting was extended to anyone who was unable to vote in person in 1985 but voters had to provide electoral registration administrators with the reason that an absent vote was required. In 2001 voters no longer had to provide a reason and any voter could apply for an absent vote on demand.

1. INTRODUCTION

This paper gives a history of the Parliamentary franchise and shows the incremental stages which led to universal suffrage across the UK by drawing on several of the recognised sources which have dealt with the subject and by referring to the key legislation.

Universal adult suffrage is considered a corner stone of a modern democracy but in the UK universal suffrage for Parliamentary elections is less than a century old. Gradual extensions of the franchise occurred in the nineteenth century but ancient distinctions between county and borough franchises persisted for some time.

The constituent parts of the United Kingdom also had different Parliamentary franchises and these were not unified until 1884.

The first general election where some women were permitted to vote was in 1918. Women were not granted equality with men in terms of the Parliamentary franchise until May 1929.

The principle of one person one vote is even younger as plural voting was only finally abolished in 1948. Plural or dual voting was possible because of business and university qualifications to vote but the *Representation of the People Act 1948* explicitly stated for the first time that each person could exercise only one vote in a Parliamentary election.

Until relatively recently in British history the extension of the vote to all men, let alone women, was actively opposed by many who thought the vote should be restricted to those of influence and means. Professor Robert Blackburn noted that:

> Even in the nineteenth century the idea of democracy, in the sense of equal political rights and universal suffrage, was still regarded by most as a dangerous experiment and subversive to any sound system of government.[1]

The opportunities to vote in general elections before the Great Reform Act were limited further by the fact that contested seats were far fewer in number than seats where a MP was returned unopposed.

In the general election of 1831 there were 658 seats available in 380 constituencies (most constituencies in England returned two MPs per seat). Of those 380 seats only one third saw a contested election. The remaining two thirds returned Members without the need for a ballot to be held.[2]

After the redistribution of seats in 1832, in the reformed House of Commons, the total number of seats remained at 658 until 1868. In the first election after the Great Reform the number of uncontested seats dropped to 189 (28%) but then rose to 275 (42%) in 1835, 236 (36%) in 1837 and 337 (51%) in 1841.[3]

These levels fluctuated through the nineteenth century, with the lowest number of uncontested seats in 1885 (6%) and the most (58%) in 1859. Even in 1910 nearly a quarter of the 670 seats returned an MP unopposed.[4]

The table below show the proportion of the total UK population that was registered to vote at Parliamentary elections since the Great Reform Act of 1832.

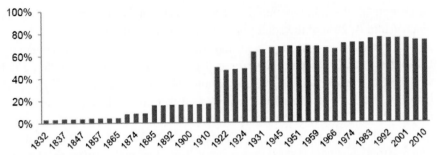

Provided by the House of Commons Social and General Statistics Research Section

Notes: (a) Figures for 1918 and earlier are for all Ireland. (b) 1910 electorate is for December 1910 General Election. (c) 1918 population figure does not include the non-civilian population of England and Wales. (d) 1974 electorate is for October 1974 General Election.

Sources: Rallings and Thrasher, *British Electoral Facts: 1832-2006* House of Commons Library RP10/36 *General Election 2010* Office for National Statistics B.R. Mitchell, *British Historical Statistics*.

Percentage of population registered to vote at general elections,1832-2010.

The main jumps in numbers of registered voters are associated with the main Reform Acts of 1832, 1867 and 1884, the extension of the Parliamentary franchise to some women in 1918 and the equal franchise Act of 1928 which granted women and men the Parliamentary franchise on an equal basis.

Estimates vary, but the Great Reform Act of 1832 probably increased the total electorate by over 50%. In 1831, the total electorate of Great Britain and Ireland was about 516,000 and this had increased to about 809,000 by 1833.[5] Despite what appeared to be a significant increase still only 3% of the total population could register to vote at Parliamentary elections. The Parliamentary franchise was largely linked to property rights rather than residence which generally meant only the affluent could qualify.

The Second Reform Act of 1867 more than doubled the number of voters in the Parliamentary boroughs by including some of the urban working classes,[6] but the increase in the county franchise was more modest. The Act meant that over 16% of the adult population (those who had reached the age of majority of 21), about 2.2 million, could register to vote.[7]

Following the Third Reform Act of 1884 the differences between the Parliamentary franchises in the boroughs and the counties remained but the qualifications for each were unified across the United Kingdom for the first time. The main beneficiaries were the agricultural working classes and the proportion of the adult population able to vote in Parliamentary elections reached almost 29% of the adult population, nearly 5 million.[8]

Universal male suffrage and the first granting of the Parliamentary franchise to some women followed the *Representation of the People Act 1918* and took the proportion of the population able to vote to 50%. The age of majority at this stage was still 21 but women were only allowed to register if they were 30 years old and separate qualifications were applied to women. Men could register as long as they were resident and property qualifications (apart from business votes) were abolished for male suffrage. Special provision was also made for armed forces voters because of the Great War and men serving in the armed forces aged 19 and 20 were allowed to register to vote.

Universal suffrage at the age of 21 was granted in 1928 following the passing of the *Representation of the People (Equal Franchise) Act 1928*. The extension of the vote to 18 year olds in 1969 took the proportion of the population able to vote to 71% with the majority of those unable to vote being children; there were other categories of people prohibited from registering (see Section 12 below).

2. ANCIENT VOTING RIGHTS IN ENGLAND

The origins of the English Parliament lay with the witans of the early kings of Anglo-Saxon England but these were not representative meetings of elected representatives. Witans were councils of noblemen and clergy who attended the king to give advice, pass legislation and discuss policy. The first occurrence of the word 'parliament' is in an official document dated 1236.[9] These early Parliaments were an extension of the king's council and were also attended by earls, barons, bishops, abbots and priors.

The earliest evidence of the king summoning representatives of the counties was in 1254 and the boroughs in 1265. Their presence was required to consent to taxation and this occurred only rarely before 1290; the earliest surviving rolls of who attended Parliament date from 1290.[10]

Ancient counties were administrative units either derived from the kingdoms of England before it was unified in the tenth century or as artificial creations from larger kingdoms. The Anglo-saxon term was 'shire' and the Norman term was 'county'.[11]

From 1290 representatives of the English counties were regularly summoned by writ to serve in Parliament and later the summoning of borough

Members also became the norm. Writs were sent to the sheriff of each county. Each county and each borough usually returned 2 Members at elections. There was no single definition of or agreement on what constituted a borough in this period. The issuing of a writ was a royal prerogative and those boroughs that became Parliamentary boroughs were usually the county town of each ancient county and a number of other important boroughs. The actual number of Parliamentary boroughs in early Parliaments fluctuated.[12]

The election of the county Members differed from that of the borough Members and the franchise eligibility within borough seats varied from borough to borough. Members were also returned for the Cinque Ports and for the Universities of Oxford and Cambridge.

Ancient voting rights in England

Restricted to males by custom rather than statute.

County franchise – freeholders of a property freehold (not restricted to land) worth 40 shillings. Every county returned MPs.

Borough franchise – Varied from borough to borough but usually dependent on residence, a property qualification/tenure or the status as a freeman or a mixture. In some boroughs the franchise was restricted to members of the corporation running the borough. Writs were only issued to certain boroughs.

University franchise – Oxford and Cambridge each had two MPs elected by members of the Senates of each university.

The first recorded return for Members of Parliament for the Cinque Ports was 1366, each returning two Members, although writs of summons were sent regularly from 1322.[13] The towns derived their right to return Members of Parliament because of their Cinque Port status and writs were issued to the Warden of the Ports rather than the county sheriffs of Kent and Sussex.

Until 1689 the Warden claimed the right to chose one of the Members.[14] Members were listed in the returns of Parliament as Cinque Port Members and not from the county in which they were situated.[15] Cinque Port Members were also sworn in separately from other borough Members,[16] but in respect of the Parliamentary franchise within the boroughs there was little difference to other Parliamentary boroughs.

From 1603 Oxford and Cambridge Universities were also granted the right to return MPs to Parliament and the method of election was different to that of the county and borough Members (see section 2.3 below).

During the period of Oliver Cromwell's rule, changes were made to the number of seats in the House of Commons and the qualifications for the franchise. There was an attempt to abolish property qualifications and extend the Parliamentary franchise but these were resisted by Cromwell. Instead, the county franchise was raised to a £200 property qualification.

The Parliamentary borough franchise remained specific to each borough but some boroughs were stripped of their right to send MPs to Parliament.[17] Those individuals identified as 'Royalists' or 'Papists' were disenfranchised.[18] Following the Restoration the changes of the Cromwell era were reversed and the election of MPs followed the pre-Civil War system until 1832.

Ancient voting rights did not specifically prohibit women's suffrage. Before 1832 the disfranchisement of women had been by custom rather than by statute but there has been little research into the subject and "it is impossible to conclude that women *never* voted".[19]

There is some evidence that there were women who believed they had the right to vote both in county and borough seats. Little is known about how single women or widows who met the property qualifications to vote in the counties were treated.[20]

Women who owned burgages in burgage boroughs or who lived in freeman boroughs[21] (see below) could influence elections. In the burgage boroughs women could transfer the vote which came with burgage ownership to a husband or male relative.[22] In some freeman boroughs the daughters of freemen could make their husbands freemen and therefore voters.[23]

A case study of the 1768 Parliamentary election in the borough of Northampton concludes that many women, not just wives of the wealthy, were involved in the pre-reform electoral process despite not actually casting votes themselves.[24] Northampton was a potwalloper borough (see section 2.2 below) where the right to vote was held by male householders. Voters had to publicly justify their household qualification and women could act as witnesses to say whether a claim to vote was truthful or not.[25] This was sometimes partisan evidence in favour of one candidate.

Where a woman was the head of the household (for example, because she was a widower or a single landlady) they could also play an important role in establishing who could vote. There were instances where a woman and her male lodger would come to an arrangement where they would trade places and the lodger would claim to be the householder in order to claim the vote.[26] The case study concludes that:

The evidence proves that women were active participants in elections, were allied to candidates, were able to gain financially from elections, and had their own vital role to play in the contest.[27]

2.1. County Franchise

The county franchise was formalised in 1430 and remained largely unaltered until the Great Reform Act of 1832 except in the county palatines of Cheshire and Durham.[28] These were administered separately and did not return Members of the English Parliament until 1545 and 1654 respectively.[29]

Before 1430 there is evidence that the right to vote for the knights of the shires in English county elections was given to "every free inhabitant householder, freeholder and non-freeholder".[30] There was no requirement for freeholders to be landed freeholders; the freehold could relate to something other than land.

The king's writs required sheriffs, who executed the writs, to hold free elections.[31] This was sometimes abused and sheriffs sometimes returned themselves or held no elections. A statute was passed in 1406 which reiterated that free elections must be held at a full shire court in full view of participants but added the requirement that writs be returned to Chancery by indenture, a form of two-part duplicate contract where each party retained half of the contract to prevent corruption.

In the late fourteenth century and early fifteenth there were calls for shire elections to be restricted to the "better folk of the shires" but the official view remained that the common assent of the whole county was required.[32] Election meetings could be large and lively and feuds between factions sometimes spilled over to election meetings.[33]

In 1429, a petition was presented to the King by the Commons which expressed concern that some elections had involved "too great and excessive number of people...of whom the greater part are by people of little or no means" and that these people "pretend[ed] to have an equivalent voice...as the most worthy knights or esquires dwelling in the same counties".[34] The petition called for the vote to be restricted to those freeholders resident in a county with a freehold value of 40 shillings a year. A freehold was not restricted to land; it could refer to many types of property.

The petition led, in 1430, to such a statute being passed and all leaseholders, regardless of the value of their leased land, were stripped of the vote. The 40 shilling resident freeholder requirement for the county franchise remained until 1832 although the interpretation of what constituted a freehold was extended in the intervening years, and the residency requirement gradually became obsolete.[35]

The Parliamentary franchise was abused by some freeholders and from the seventeenth century the 'faggot' vote became a common form of electoral abuse. Freeholders would subdivide large freeholdings into smaller 40 shilling freeholds purely to create so-called 'faggot' voters, who would then vote as the primary freeholder wished. A statute was passed in 1696, dubbed the Splitting Act, with the intention of preventing the faggot vote but the Act was interpreted loosely and the practice continued.[36]

The county franchise was extended to clergymen of the Church of England and some offices connected with the judiciary system at the end of the seventeenth century.[37]

The proportion of the population able to vote in Parliamentary elections to elect county Members varied. The total across England (including Monmouthshire) was an estimated number of voters of 176,800 out of a population of about 13.1 million (1.35%)

In 1831, just before the reforms of the Great Reform Act, Middlesex had a population of 1,358,330 and an estimated electorate of 3,000 (0.22%) but in Herefordshire the figures were an estimated 4,000 voters from a population of 111,211 (3.6%).[38]

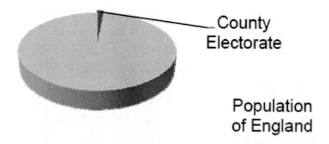

County Electorate

Population of England

2.2. Borough Franchise

There were no set criteria for which towns and cities were represented in Parliament but early writs were generally issued to larger boroughs. Members returned from boroughs had to be paid from local funds and this was often seen as burdensome by the local electorate. Several boroughs which returned

Members in early Parliaments managed to avoid being summoned in subsequent Parliaments.

Before the industrial revolution, which was centred in the north, the industrial life of England had been concentrated in the south. Cornwall with its mineral wealth, particularly tin, and Wiltshire and Somerset's wool industry were renowned before Lancashire gained prominence for its cotton.[39] As a consequence southern boroughs were more numerous than northern boroughs. Royal patronage was also stronger in the south; fifteen new Parliamentary boroughs were created in the Duchy of Cornwall from the time of Henry VIII to the end of the Elizabethan age.

There was no uniform borough franchise across England. Various commentators have grouped the English boroughs into four main types of franchise, but even within these groups there was a variety of restrictions and qualifications placed on eligibility to vote. Some boroughs combined groups to define the local electorate. There was no systematic form of electoral registration.

The rotten and pocket boroughs closely associated with the reforms of 1832 came from all categories of Parliamentary borough. A rotten borough was one where the electorate had decreased significantly or had ceased to exist at all but where the right to return MPs to Parliament had been retained.[40] The most notorious example was Old Sarum, which had no resident electorate. Pocket boroughs were those where the election of an MP was controlled by one person or family.[41]

Whether county or borough seats, all elections were conducted in public and votes were cast in public by each voter. Poll books were kept and patrons could see who voted for which candidate.

'Scot and Lot' and 'Potwaioper' Boroughs

The scot and lot qualification was based on the householder's payment (scot) of a share (lot) of local poor and church rates.[42] The potwalloper qualification was a householder who was self-sustaining (they made no claim on poor relief) and who had their own hearth on which they could cook or boil (wallop) a pot.

The electorates in these boroughs were like the county electorates before the introduction of the 40 shilling requirement as the vote was dependent on residence and not on wealth or income from a freehold.[43]

Large scot and lot boroughs, like Westminster, were among the most open as there were too many voters for candidates or patrons to influence all the votes. Westminster had an unusually large electorate of about 17,000 in

1816.[44] Smaller boroughs, however, were just as open to influence at election times as some of the other types of borough. Tregony, in Cornwall, had a potwalloper electorate of about 260 in 1831, but many relied on the bribes they received at election time for their main income and many homes were built purely for the purposes of electoral gain.[45]

Burgage Boroughs

A burgage was land and/or property tenure in a town for which payment was usually made to the king or a lord by the exchange of money rather than services.[46] Burgages existed in most towns regardless of whether the town had the right to return MPs to Parliament. In those Parliamentary boroughs where burgage formed the basis of the franchise there was no uniform set of conditions on how the franchise was granted, it was down to individual boroughs to determine.

Most burgage boroughs had small electorates but these did not necessarily need to be permanently resident. Some boroughs required electors to be resident for a set number of days before the election and in the case of Bedwin, in Wiltshire, it was the custom to let burgage houses four or five days before an election.[47]

With small electorates and burgage tenures which could be acquired, it was easy for wealthy men to control the votes within these Parliamentary boroughs. The most famous of these was the Parliamentary borough of Old Sarum, which had been the site of the earliest settlements of Salisbury. The burgage that gave the franchise in Old Sarum was a ploughed field.[48]

According to *The Times* in 1830 there was "no house nor vestige of a house" within the Parliamentary borough of Old Sarum.[49] Formal election proceedings were conducted in a temporary building under a tree,[50] but contested elections were almost unheard of and Old Sarum was "an extreme example of a rotten borough for almost its entire representative history". [51] Immediately before its abolition in 1832, the seat returned two brothers as MPs.

The Alexander brothers had owned all 11 burgages within Old Sarum since 1820 and had returned themselves as the two MPs for the borough at each general election from that year.[52]

Freeman Boroughs

Freeman status was originally an ancient status which meant a man was not bound by serfdom to a local lord. When early boroughs were granted charters many made references to freemen, who also had to undertake municipal duties, and the status of a freeman was incorporated into the rules governing the Parliamentary franchise within some Parliamentary boroughs.[53]

In early borough charters freemen were usually resident but, as a seat in Parliament became more prestigious, many freeman boroughs extended freeman status, and therefore the vote, to non-residents.

In Gloucester, for example, freedom of the city could be acquired by birth, apprenticeship, gift or purchase. Between 1820 and 1832 over 800 freemen were created. Of these 504 were by birth and of the rest, 183 were by honorary gift, with the rest split between apprenticeships and purchased freedoms. Nearly half of all the freemen created in that period (366) were created in 1830, the year of a contested election, and about two-thirds of the new freemen were non-resident.[54]

Corporation Boroughs

These were boroughs where the corporation governing a borough held the power to elect the Members of Parliament. Before a seat in Parliament became prestigious or desired, some corporations elected their Members of Parliament with little consideration of the residents of the borough.[55] Some boroughs even allowed their right to return MPs to Parliament lapse.

In 1444 an Act of Parliament was passed stating that all borough elections should be held in the borough where the writ had been sent (previously the final stages of borough elections took place in county courts overseen by a sheriff).[56] This Act also stated that the election of Members of Parliament should be by citizens and burgesses and anyone replacing a duly elected candidate with their own choice would have to pay the king and the replaced candidate compensation. Many borough corporations declined to pass on the decision of choosing the MPs to the local electorate. Several corporation boroughs persisted until the reforms of 1832.[57]

The Parliamentary borough of Tiverton returned MPs to Parliament from 1621. The corporation controlling the borough numbered 25 men and the corporation was entirely self-perpetuating. The 25 corporation members were all nominees of the local patron and the Parliamentary franchise was limited to the 25 members of the corporation (the population in 1831 was 9,776).[58]

2.3. University Representation

Oxford and Cambridge Universities had their own representation in Parliament from 1603. Both universities had petitioned for direct representation in the House of Commons before then to represent their interests in legislation directly affecting them.

In 1603 the privilege of sending two Members of Parliament from each of the two universities was granted. The cost of sending the Members to Parliament was borne by the universities themselves.

The franchise was granted to members of the Senate of each university and was not based on ownership or occupation of a property and nor was residency in Oxford or Cambridge a requirement. Bishops, peers and minors who were members of the Senate were barred from voting. The Senates of each University numbered 500.[59]

Vice-Chancellors acted as returning officers and unusually, voting was conducted in secret. There was little evidence of corruption in university seats and at Oxford candidates were not allowed to canvas and were even forbidden from coming within ten miles of the university when a poll was pending.[60]

3. OTHER PRE-1832 PARLIAMENTARY FRANCHISES

3.1. Wales

Welsh representation in Parliament dates back to the sixteenth century. There is evidence that writs were issued in 1322 and 1327 to Edmund, Earl of Arundell and Justiciary of Wales, to send 24 men to Parliament to assist in the last Parliament summoned by Edward II.[61] This did not set a precedent and regular representation for Wales did not occur until the reign of Henry VIII.

In this period two Acts of Union were passed to enfranchise the Principality and establish the ancient counties of Wales. The legislation was passed in 1536 but writs were not sent to Wales until 1542.[62]

From the sixteenth century until the reforms of 1832, Wales returned 24 MPs to the House of Commons. Each of the 12 counties were represented by one Member each, with the remaining 12 MPs representing Parliamentary boroughs. The Parliamentary boroughs were the county towns in each county except Merionethshire. No borough within Meirionnydd was considered suitable as a Parliamentary borough and the twelfth borough seat was granted to Haverfordwest in Pembrokeshire, in addition to Pembroke. Monmouthshire, which at this time included the Newport and Gwent area, was considered separate to the Welsh counties.

In the reign of Henry VIII the duty of sending a knight of the shire to Westminster, and paying his expenses, was regarded as a financial burden and this may be the reason that the Welsh counties were only required to send one MP. In relation to the English counties the counties in Wales were comparatively less affluent.[63]

Ancient voting rights in Wales

Wales granted seats in Parliament in the sixteenth century on a similar basis to England.

County franchise was the same as England but required the creation of the ancient counties of Wales.

Borough franchise – no uniform borough franchise but many boroughs created at this time were corporation boroughs. Parliamentary franchise extended to contributory boroughs so many borough MPs represented more than one borough.

No university constituencies.

The county franchise in Wales was the same as in the English shires. In 1536 an Act was passed that made provision for the establishment of the ancient counties of Wales and their county towns, and stated that law and justice was to be administered as in England.[64] This Act also provided that the method of election for the county and borough Members to be returned to Parliament should be in the same manner as in "other shires of this realm".[65] This meant that the 40 shilling franchise was transferred directly to the Welsh counties.

As mentioned above, there was no uniform franchise in the English boroughs to transfer across to the Welsh boroughs. In the time of Henry VIII many new boroughs were corporation boroughs.

A second Act during Henry VIII's reign extended the Parliamentary franchise to contributory boroughs in several counties.[66] These were boroughs which were granted the right to participate in the election of the county towns' borough Member of Parliament.[67] The second Act stipulated that the right to contribute to the election of the Member of Parliament went hand in hand with the liability to the Member of Parliament's wages. Although wages were probably not paid in most cases the principle led to most Parliamentary boroughs in Wales enfranchising inhabitant freemen.

Welsh boroughs were more open seats than some of the English boroughs. The electorates were generally large, comparatively, and those seats split between contributory boroughs had scattered electorates. It meant patrons were less secure than their English counterparts.[68]

3.2. Scotland

Scottish representation in the Parliament of Great Britain was determined by the Treaty of Union agreed between Scotland and England in 1706. The Acts of Union in the separate Scottish and English Parliaments ratified the treaty and took effect in May 1707.

The treaty agreed that Scotland would have 45 MPs and 16 Lords in the new Parliament of Great Britain. The English Commission negotiating the treaty had wanted to grant Scotland 38 MPs but the Scottish Commission had requested more. In the end the English Commission proposed 45 MPs "and no more", an offer accepted by the Scottish Commission.[69]

The Scottish Parliament was a unicameral Parliament which, by 1707, comprised three 'estates'; Nobles, burgesses and shire commissioners. There were also a small number of ex officio officers of state who were Members of the Parliament.

There had been a fourth estate, higher clergy and bishops, but these had been excluded since 1690.[70] In 1706, the Scottish Parliament had 67 borough (known as burghs) Members and 83 Members from the 33 counties. Peers and their eldest sons were excluded from burgh seats.

The method of election of the 45 MPs to serve in the House of Commons was left to the Scottish Parliament to determine. In the first Parliament of Great Britain in 1707 a delegation of 45 MPs was chosen from the sitting Members (commissioners) of the Scottish Parliament, in part to avoid elections in Scotland from producing an anti-Union majority. They joined the English Parliament which had been elected in 1705 to create the new British Parliament.[71]

The Scottish Parliament had decided that thereafter 30 county representatives and 15 burgh representatives should be elected to serve in the House of Commons in Westminster, and that "none shall elect, nor be elected to represent a shire or burgh...except such as are now capable by the laws of this kingdom to elect or be elected as commissioners for shire or burgh".[72]

County Franchise

The county franchise in Scotland was held by 40 shilling freeholders of 'old extent', an old valuation which was effectively uprated. In England the 40 shilling franchise was fixed from 1430 and gradually more men came within the 40 shilling bracket. In Scotland, however, the number of county voters remained small. In 1831 the population of Scotland was about 2,380,000. The county electorate was estimated to be 2,380, or 0.10% of the population.[73]

Many of the county voters would have had little direct contact with the land that gave rise to the freehold franchise. Scottish law allowed for the land to be sold but with landowner retaining a 'superiority', or feudal right, over the freehold. The superiority became little more than a piece of parchment that could be easily bought and sold.[74]

Ancient voting rights in Scotland

Scotland granted seats in UK Parliament as part of the Acts of Union of 1707

County franchise similar to that of England, based on 40 shilling freeholders, but in Scotland the value of the freeholding was uprated which meant that the number of those who qualified for the vote remained small (in contrast to England where the 40 shilling valuation was not uprated and as more people could afford a 40 shilling freehold the number of electors began to grow).

Royal burgh franchise was vested in the unelected burgh corporations so there was effectively no real electorate.

No university constituencies.

Royal Burgh Franchise

Royal burgh representatives were chosen by unelected burgh councils. These had originally been elected annually by freemen of the burghs but from 1469 members of an existing council chose the members of next council. The councils therefore became self-perpetuating.

There were no rotten boroughs, as in England, because all royal burghs were real towns liable to paying royal taxation. Commissioners from the burghs also had to be merchants or craftsmen from the burgh which meant the burghs were less likely to be overtaken by the gentry.[75]

After the Union 65 of the 66 royal burghs (Edinburgh was exempt) were grouped into 14 districts of burghs, similar to the Welsh groupings. Unlike the Welsh boroughs, elections were not conducted directly by the electorate in the primary borough. Instead, in Scotland, burgh councils would send a delegate from each contributory burgh to a convention at the presiding burgh to select the MP. Delegates were not required to vote as instructed and in the event of a tie, the presiding burgh's delegate cast the deciding vote.[76]

3.3. Ireland

The Irish Parliament more closely resembled the English Parliament, particularly after Henry VIII became the king of all Ireland. It was a bicameral Parliament with a House of Lords and a House of Commons. Membership in early Parliaments fluctuated as the number of counties and boroughs that returned MPs varied. This was because the areas that were loyal to the king of England, who ruled Ireland by virtue of the feudal title of Lord of Ireland, varied over time.

From the time Henry VIII was declared king of all Ireland, in 1541, the number of Parliamentary boroughs grew and from 1690 the Irish House of Commons was steady at 300 MPs from 150 two-Member constituencies. These came from the 32 counties, 117 Parliamentary boroughs and Trinity College, Dublin. Membership of the Irish House of Lords also increased with a number of Irish peerages created, although many of them were permanently absent.[77]

Disfranchising Catholics

The Parliamentary franchise in the Irish counties was specifically withheld from Roman Catholics by statute from 1727 to 1793. The restriction was one of a number placed on Catholics during the period. [78] In Ireland this effectively barred about 80% of the male adult population in the counties of Ireland from exercising the vote in Parliamentary elections.[79]

Restrictions on Catholics voting in borough Parliamentary elections had been in place before 1727 under local by-laws.[80] Earlier restrictions had been placed on Catholic voters by requiring that they should take discriminatory oaths of allegiance and abjuration before being allowed to vote.[81]

Other restrictions had been designed to prevent Catholics taking public office, including Catholic peers and MPs in the Irish Parliament. In order to take their seats MPs and peers had to take an oath abrogating the supremacy of the Pope and make a declaration that transubstantiation did not occur at the Last Supper.[82] Catholic peers continued to be summoned to Parliament but could not make such a declaration and as a result, from 1692 until its abolition in 1800, the Irish Parliament was a Protestant assembly. Catholics continued to be barred from sitting in the UK Parliament until 1829 when the *Roman Catholic Relief Act 1829* made it lawful for any Roman Catholic to sit and vote in either House of Parliament (with the exception of Roman Catholic priests who were prevented from standing for election to the House of Commons).[83]

County Franchise

The electorate for the Irish counties and boroughs was similar to that of England. The county franchise was originally based on the 40 shilling freehold qualification. Shortly before Union and the abolition of the Irish Parliament in 1800, the county franchise was reformed by an Act that also revised electoral administration and registration. Three types of freehold were specified for qualification to register to vote.[84] The county franchise was further revised post-Union. In 1829, the *Irish Franchise Act* raised the threshold for eligibility for the county franchise from 40 shillings (£2) to £10. The result was that the registered county electorate fell by about 80%.[85] Estimates varied but the county franchise dropped from around 215,000 across Ireland to under 40,000.[86]

Ancient voting rights in Ireland

Ireland granted seats in UK Parliament following the Union of 1800 and the abolition of the Irish Parliament.

County franchise originally similar to that of England, based on 40 shilling freeholders, but reformed shortly before Union. Further revised in 1829 by raising the threshold from 40 shillings to £10 which drastically reduced the electorate.

Borough franchise had a similar mix of property, freeman or corporation electorates but the qualification levels differed to England and many freemen were non-resident. Post-Union the largest 31 boroughs were granted the status of Parliamentary boroughs. No grouping of boroughs as in Scotland and Wales.

Trinity College, Dublin had one MP with an electorate of nearly 100 fellows and scholars.

Registration in order to vote, requiring the voter's proof of property qualifications, was established in Ireland earlier than England to prevent county landlords converting leases for electoral gain. However, this was not foolproof; the certificate gained on registration was valid for eight years and not always surrendered when voters moved away or died. This led to instances of electoral abuse including personation, a crime almost unknown in England at this time.[87] It also sometimes gave potential candidates the opportunity to examine an up-to-date register to see whether or not it was worth the expense of becoming a candidate at an election by analysing the likely loyalties of those registered.[88]

Borough Franchise

The Union of Ireland and Great Britain to form the United Kingdom of Great Britain and Ireland followed a different pattern than the Union between Scotland and England. There were no Commissions and less Parliamentary scrutiny.[89]

The Articles of Union provided for 32 Irish Members of the House of Lords and 100 Irish Members of the House of Commons of the new United Kingdom Parliament. The Irish seats in the House of Commons were to comprise two Members each from the 32 counties, two each from Dublin and Cork and one Member from Trinity College, Dublin. The University electorate for Trinity College comprised 22 fellows and 70 scholars.[90]

The remaining 31 MPs were to come from the largest 31 boroughs, based on taxable wealth, across Ireland which meant a significant number of Parliamentary boroughs that had had representation in the Irish Parliament would be merged into the counties.

A system of grouping boroughs, as in Scotland, was considered but rejected.[91] In what is now Northern Ireland there were 10 boroughs. In order of size these were Belfast, Newry, Londonderry, Armagh, Lisburne, Downpatrick, Coleraine, Dungannon, Enniskillien and Carrickfergus.

The Parliamentary boroughs had the same mix of voting qualifications as the English boroughs in the English Parliament. Post-Union boroughs were a mixture of corporation boroughs, freeman boroughs (not necessarily resident), 'county-boroughs' (seats where burgesses, freemen and 40 shilling freeholders combined to make the electorate) and boroughs with a £5 householder property qualification. In boroughs where freemen were entitled to vote many freemen were non-resident and freeman status was often given by special favour. As a result Catholics made up a very small proportion of the electorate. As in England, many boroughs were controlled by family or corporation interests and in many of the seats it was non-Irish families exerting the control.[92]

It consists of detailed studies of elections and electoral politics in each constituency, and of closely researched accounts of the lives of everyone who was elected to Parliament in the period, together with surveys drawing out the themes and discoveries of the research and adding information on the operation of Parliament as an institution.

The volumes on *The House of Commons, 1820-1832,* available online, gives details of each Parliamentary borough in existence before the Great Reform Act. For each borough the number of voters and the qualification in order to vote are given. Entries detail elections, how the choice of MP was influenced within the borough and the effects of the Great Reform Act.

Below is an extract for the borough constituency of Westminster.

Background Information

Right of Election: in inhabitants paying scot and lot

Estimated number qualified to vote: about 13,000

Number of voters: 9,280 in 1820

Population: 182,796 (1821); 202,460 (1831)

While a significant proportion of the electorate were members of the leisured classes, including many of the social and political elite, and of the legal profession (probably about 19 per cent in total), it has been calculated that by 1820 about 66 per cent were tradesmen, craftsmen, skilled artisans and shopkeepers involved in the production or sale (sometimes, of course, in both) of consumer goods for a thriving market. There were comparatively few poor labourers and menials, but the potentially violent mob was a factor in Westminster politics.

4. GREAT REFORM ACT OF 1832

The *Representation of the People Act 1832*, known as the Great Reform Act, reformed the distribution of seats in England and Wales.[93] Separate Reform Acts were introduced to cover Ireland and Scotland.

4.1. England and Wales

The Act was famous for disfranchising boroughs such as Old Sarum and creating new seats, particularly in the industrial towns of the north of England. The number of county seats was also increased by either splitting a county into two divisions or by granting an additional Member to represent the whole county. The Act also reformed the Parliamentary franchise and, for the first time in England and Wales, introduced the first systematic of registration of eligible voters.

Parliamentary reform was a significant issue at this time. On the failure of a previous Reform Bill there was rioting across the country and there was a real sense of crisis as the successful Bill made its way through Parliament. The King was prepared, although not keen, to create up to 50 peers to make sure the Bill succeeded in the House of Lords, the government of Lord Grey resigned and there was the threat of a mass uprising if reform was not carried in some form.[94]

Despite such controversies the Act was never an attempt to build a new electoral system, nor to simplify the existing one. The main change was the redistribution of seats in favour of northern industrial boroughs, but some boroughs remained in the control of wealthy families and electoral malpractice persisted.

The county and borough franchises remained different and based largely on property holding, which meant that the extension of the vote was modest. And far from simplifying the Parliamentary franchise, the 1832 Act complicated the situation by introducing new categories of franchise and increasing the number of restrictions on eligibility.

The Act was the first time that legislation had specifically limited the vote to male householders by stating that "every male person of full age and not subject to any legal incapacity" (and who fulfilled the various other requirements) was entitled to register to vote. Before 1832 the exclusion of women from Parliamentary elections was based on custom and some women might have voted at the parish level elections. Local government voters in incorporated boroughs in England and Wales were restricted after 1835 by the Municipal Corporations Act 1835 (5&^ William IV, chapter 86) to registered burgesses of each borough (section XXIX) who by virtue of section IX had to be "male persons". [95]

County Franchise

The 40 shilling freehold qualification was retained for the county franchise for those with inherited freeholds; it continued to be applied to all types of freehold income not just land. Those 40 shilling freeholders who held the freehold tenure for life had restrictions placed on them (Section XVIII of the Act).[96]

Two new categories of property based franchise were created and one new category based on occupancy.

The property based categories extended the Parliamentary franchise to £10 copyholders (Section XIX) and £10 leaseholders (Section XX). The copyholders were an ancient form of tenant; they held their tenure from a lord of a manor and the name derived from the copy of the tenure copyholders held which matched a court held record of the tenure. The value of the land had to be at least £10 in order to qualify for the vote.

The £10 leasehold franchise was granted to those with a lease of at least 60 years and a property valued at £10. For those with a lease between 20 and 60 years the value had to be £50.

Section XX of the Act, by virtue of the so-called Chandos amendment, named after the Marquess of Chandos, also enfranchised those who rented and were resident in a property, as long as the rent was not less than £50 per year. The inclusion of these £50 tenants-at-will was criticised by some reformers as it would enable landlords to control more votes.[97] These voters, however, may have been as independent as any other county elector.[98]

Borough Franchise

The new borough franchise was based on occupancy of property. Male householders who were of age (21 years old) and who had occupied a property worth £10 for at least 12 months could vote if they were duly registered (see below). The property could be a house, warehouse, counting-house, shop, or other building as long as it was occupied. The land/property had to be within the Parliamentary borough boundaries and had to have been rated, with the householder having paid all rates and taxes.[99]

The 1832 Act was the first to explicitly state that the householder had to be male.

A potential borough voter was barred from registering if they had been in receipt of local poor relief in the preceding 12 months (Section XXXVI)., a restriction not applied to county voters until 1867.

The franchises of burgesses and freemen that existed in the boroughs before 1832 were allowed to continue for the lifetime of existing voters in most cases, as long as they remained resident and registered their vote (except in those Parliamentary boroughs that were abolished by the Act). This initially benefited poorer existing voters but as they died the franchise became socially narrower.[100]

Electoral Registration

The 1832 Act introduced the first system of electoral registration in England and Wales. An earlier attempt had been made to create an electoral register of those eligible to exercise the county franchise in 1788 when an Act was passed to allow qualifying freeholders to enroll and for county lists to be published. In 1789 the Act was repealed following the submission of a number of petitions to Parliament. Most of the petitions were principally concerned with the prohibitive costs of implementing the legislation.[101]

In some counties a system of registration had grown up in an attempt to ensure only true electors could cast their vote, but the system was not effective nor fool proof. Boroughs generally had small and well known electorates and any attempt at personation would have been difficult.[102]

The 1832 Act effectively made the eligibility to vote in Parliamentary elections dependent on having your name on the electoral register. The other qualifications to vote mentioned above were still required but potential voters had to prove these requirements in order to gain a place on the register and a fee of 1 shilling had to be paid.[103]

The process of registration was complicated and many people qualified to vote did not bother to register. This led to a new form of electoral abuse, where electoral agents would register apathetic potential voters in return for assurances of the newly registered voters casting their vote for the agents' patron (votes were still cast in public at open meetings).[104]

Registration was revised in 1843 when an Act was passed to increase the registration of voters by improving the performance of the overseers who compiled the list. The Act also allowed potential voters more time to pay their rates to avoid disqualification from registering and it allowed barristers who heard objections to someone's inclusion on a register to force costs to be paid by the objector in cases that were deemed vexatious.[105] The measures made little difference.[106]

In 1864 a Committee of MPs reported that:

> Your Committee have found the most unanimous opinion of the witnesses examined to be, that the present system of county registration is faulty inasmuch as:

> The registers are at once impure and defective; and where, and so far as these evils are remedied, the process is frequently attended with annoyance and expense to individuals.
>
> Great facilities are afforded for placing or continuing upon the register of a county the names of people not qualified to vote.[107]

Legislation followed but problems persisted. It was considered a normal part of the election process for party agents to submit blanket objections to peoples' inclusion on the electoral register across a constituency. This was in the knowledge that a significant number of qualified voters would fail to turn up in court to defend their place on the register and they would therefore be removed.[108] In 1878 an Act was passed that included a provision to allow, but did not compel, Parliamentary boroughs to register Parliamentary voters differently. Before then registers were compiled on a parish basis and alphabetically.[109] Section 21 of the 1878 Act gave boroughs the option of compiling registers in the same way as municipal registers were compiled, in street order using rate books, but the registers remained separate.[110] Other changes to the methods and outcomes of objections were made. A Registration Act followed the major reforms of 1885 (see below) which extended the provisions of the 1878 Act to the counties.[111]

The passage of time, the statutory modifications and the increase in party organisation, which in the latter years of the nineteenth century had led to local party organisations systematically and thoroughly registering their supporters, gradually led to improved, although not perfect, registers of electors.[112]

It should be noted that the registration of votes for municipal and Parliamentary elections was separate until the middle of the twentieth century:

> The essential difference between the two franchises related to payment of local rates. For nineteenth-century reformers there was a critical relationship between taxation and representation. Various Acts defining the franchise were quite specific about the need to maintain this link between payment for local services and the power to elect stewards of such budgets.[113]

Main changes of the 1832 Reform Act

Voter registration introduced for Parliamentary elections for the first time. County franchise retained for 40 shilling freeholders but extended to other property based qualifications (£10 copy holders and £10 leaseholders).

Extended to tenants as long as the property being rented was worth £50.

Borough franchises extended to householders in properties worth £10. Ancient voting rights retained in most cases as long as voter was resident in the borough. Those in receipt of poor relief prevented from registering to vote.

The first legislation to limit explicitly the Parliamentary franchise to male householders.

Redistribution of Parliamentary seats – new Parliamentary boroughs created, some boroughs abolished and many counties divided but definition of boundaries left to a separate Act (*Parliamentary Boundaries Act 1832*, 2 and 3 William IV, chapter 64)

4.2. Effects of the 1832 Act

The Great Reform Act increased the electorate of Britain from about 509,000 to about 721,000, an increase of over 40%. However, the total number of adults who could vote was still less than 8% of the adult population (over the age of 21). The main classes of voters added to the total were small landowners, tenant farmers and shopkeepers.[114]

The rise in the electorate nationally concealed some significant variations in the effects of the Act.[115] In the English boroughs, the electorate rose by about 61%, from 168,298 in 1831 to 270,639 in 1832, although the lack of voter registration before 1832 makes the figures approximate.[116] The lack of contested elections in the period also makes the accuracy of some pre-registration electorates uncertain.

Three quarters of this rise was as a result of the creation of new Parliamentary boroughs.[117] Some of the most significant increases in the electorate were in boroughs where the borough corporation formed the electorate or tightly controlled those eligible to vote. Bath is the most extreme example where the electorate rose from 30 in 1830 to 2,329 in 1832.[118]

In some of the boroughs that retained their right to return MPs, the electorate actually fell as a result of the Reform Act. This was particularly the case in places where non-resident freeman had previously been eligible to vote but who were disfranchised by the residence requirement. Some of the 'potwalloper' boroughs such as Preston, where male suffrage was generally much wider, saw a decrease in electorates as poorer voters no longer fulfilled the requirement to qualify for a vote, or could not or would not pay the fee to register.[119]

The county electorate saw a more modest increase in the electorate, from an estimated 266,232 in 1830 to 344,015 in 1832, an increase of 29%. As with the borough electorates the lack of registration and contested elections makes the pre-1832 figures approximate. The county electorate in Wales as a whole saw a similar level of increase with a 27.5% increase of the electorate from 19,936 to 25,462.[120]

In some counties the electorate decreased in size. This was in part because of the number of new Parliamentary boroughs created, which therefore no longer contributed to the county electorate. Yorkshire, for example, saw the creation of 7 new Parliamentary boroughs (a net increase of 4) which included Leeds, Bradford and Sheffield. The county electorate across the three Ridings of Yorkshire declined by 34% (nearly 17,000).[121]

As with the boroughs, some of the reduction across England and Wales was due to the unwillingness of potential voters to register. As well as the requirement to pay to register many voters refused to register as they did not see why they had to, having never needed to register in the past.[122]

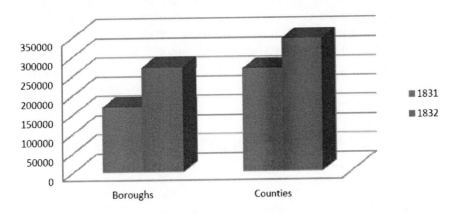

Change in English electorate 1831-32.

The continuation of property qualifications for voting meant that plural voting continued to be possible. An elector might be entitled to a university vote as well as a residential vote. The inclusion of business premises meant that some people could qualify for a business vote and a residential vote. Some men even qualified for all three but in cases where a voter was entitled to a business vote and a university vote he could only use one of them.[123]

However, if someone qualified for a residential vote in more than one seat he was able to exercise both votes.

The Great Reform Act of 1832 was seen by many as an Act to settle once and for all the question of the Parliamentary franchise. The Tory Party considered it a "final and irrevocable settlement of a great constitutional question".[124] Others saw it as doing no more than was necessary and its supporters saw it as a remedy to the many ills of the system that existed before 1832.[125]

In reality its achievements were modest. The worst of the rotten boroughs were abolished but according to Hostettler and Block, 70 boroughs continued to be controlled by patrons and wide disparities remained between the electorates of the smallest and largest seats, which meant small boroughs had the same influence as new boroughs like Manchester.[126]

The Reform Act also failed to eliminate corrupt practices at elections. Bribery and corruption continued and the lack of a secret ballot meant intimidation was easy.[127] The abolition of closed boroughs and creation of new electorates meant greater opportunities to bribe new electors.[128] Treating increased after the Reform Act,[129] and violence and intimidation continued; voters were sometimes terrorised on polling day by hired thugs.[130] Many county landlords also managed to exert undue influence on their tenants.[131]

The complexities of the registration system led to people not registering, some through apathy, as they did not see why they should need to register, and some through cost, as the shilling payment deterred many poorer voters from registering.[132]

5. 1832 REFORMS IN SCOTLAND AND IRELAND

5.1. Scotland

One month after the passing of the Great Reform Act an equivalent Act was passed for Scotland.[133] In terms of the extension of the Parliamentary franchise this was the most significant of the three Reform Acts passed in 1832 and was less of a reform act and more of an Act of enfranchisement. Scotland had been described as resembling "one vast, rotten borough" where elections were rare and those that were held could not be described as representative.[134]

The county franchise was retained by those voters who already had the 'superiority' or parchment vote. The Parliamentary franchise was also extended in a similar way to the extension of the vote in England. It was extended to occupying freeholders of a property worth £10 and to leaseholders of property worth £10 as long as the lease was not less than 57 years; to tenants of £50 properties with a lease of at least 19 years and to those renting a property worth £50 or more.

The Parliamentary franchise in the burghs was transformed. The Act abolished the election of Members of Parliament by delegation and removed the burgh councils from the election process. The burgh franchise was the same as proposed for the rest of the United Kingdom, the £10 householder qualification.

The Act increased the number of MPs from Scotland from 45 to 53. The county representation remained at 30 MPs and the extra 8 seats were granted to the burghs but there was limited redistribution in comparison to England.

Electoral registration was also introduced by the Act, as in England, and the register had to be updated annually. A fee of two shillings was required to register. Various sections of the Act dealt with different aspects of electoral administration, such as polling times and penalties for breaches of the Act.

The Act omitted university representation for Scotland. An attempt had been made during the passage of the Bill to create two university seats with one given to St Andrews and Glasgow and the other seat to Edinburgh and Aberdeen. It was rejected because Master's degrees could be granted by Scottish universities without residence or examination and there was no true parallel with Oxford, Cambridge or Dublin.[135]

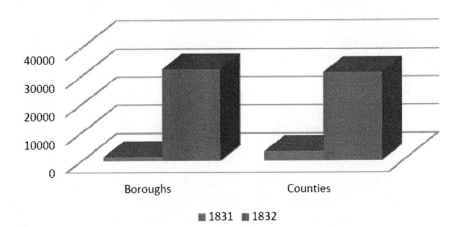

Change in Scottish electorate 1831-32.

The Scottish Reform Act had a significant impact on the size of the electorate. The county franchise rose from about 3,200 to over 31,000. The burgh franchise rose from what was effectively a self-perpetuating closed electoral system of 1,300 council members to a far more representative 32,000.[136]

5.2. Ireland

Two months after the Great Reform Act of 1832 a similar Act was passed to apply to Ireland.[137] As with the Great Reform Act it was the third version of the Bill that was eventually passed. Many of the provisions were similar to those in the Great Reform Act. Catholic emancipation and attempts to restore the 40 shilling freeholder vote from the county franchise made the Bill controversial but the need to end the monopoly of some corporations and patrons and to open up the electorate in some of the Irish boroughs meant Ireland could not be overlooked during the reforms of 1832.[138]

The county franchise remained with those who had a £10 freehold (it was not reduced to the 40 shilling level) but extensions of the county franchise were similar to those in England and Wales. A leasehold franchise was granted to those with a leasehold for life of at least 60 years and a property valued at £10, or at least 20 years and a property valued at £20; a leasehold of £10 held for at least 20 years, and £10 copyholders.[139]

The borough franchise in the county borough seats was extended to £10 freeholders, £20 leaseholders and £10 householders (whether rented or owned) who were occupants. In the county boroughs the 40 shilling qualification was retained for those who still had it.

In Parliamentary boroughs that were not administratively 'counties of themselves' the £10 householder vote applied. As in England and Wales, voters could only vote in a borough election if their qualification to vote was within a Parliamentary borough but satisfied both requirements of borough and county franchise.

The university franchise was extended to all scholars who were on Dublin University's books who were of age and had a Masters degree or higher. This raised the university electorate from nearly 90 to over 2,000.[140]

The Act applied the rules for registration to boroughs as well as counties and a fee was required to register. The Parliamentary franchise was dependent on appearing on the electoral register.

The Irish Reform Act was more modest than the English equivalent when it came to redistribution of seats. Five additional Members were created: one each for Belfast, Limerick, Waterford, Galway and the University of Dublin, but no boroughs were disfranchised. The reform of borough representation at the time of the Union with Great Britain had eradicated the rotten boroughs.

The increase in the size of the electorate in Ireland was about 19 %. The borough franchise rose from 22,603 to 29,444[141] and the county vote rose by about 8,300 to 60,500. This was still a fraction of the number entitled to vote before the abolition of the 40 shilling county franchise in 1829.

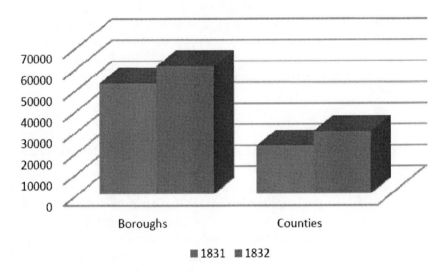

Change in the Irish electorate 1831-32.

6. THE PARLIAMENTARY VOTERS (IRELAND) ACT 1850

In 1848 a Bill was introduced to remove ambiguities within the Irish franchise and to remove the "many and grave abuses" of the registration in Ireland.[142] It was the third version of the Bill that went on to become an Act.

The purpose of the Bill was to remove ambiguities of the franchise that led to different interpretations of who could be entered on the register; barristers and Judges could not agree on who was eligible to be registered.

The Bill also made provision to extend the Parliamentary franchise. This was during the potato famine in Ireland and in introducing the Bill, in 1848, the Irish Secretary stated:

He would not weary the House by going into detail, or by alluding to figures; but documents were at the command of every hon. Member of the House to show that the constituencies of Ireland were dwindling away, and yearly becoming less; and except the House stepped in and legislated on the subject, the representative system in Ireland would become nothing more nor less than a nullity.[143]

The third stated aim of the Bill was to create a Parliamentary franchise unconnected with any tenure, but based on the rateable value of a property.

Male householders in Parliamentary boroughs in a property of a minimum rateable value £8 could register to vote at borough elections.

The county franchise was given to householders in a property with a rateable value of a minimum of £12, or £5 in fee tail property (where inheritance rights were restricted by common law).[144] The changes to borough and county electorates were expected to quadruple the numbers of voters in Ireland.[145]

7. THE SECOND REFORM ACT IN ENGLAND AND WALES

The *Representation of the People 1867* became known as the Second Reform Act.[146] Like the original Reform Act it applied only to England and Wales and separate legislation was passed for Scotland and Ireland.

Pressure for a Second Reform Act had grown almost from the passing of the Great Reform Act of 1832. This was partly in response to the continued corruption in Parliamentary elections following 1832. The general election of 1841 had such widespread corruption that the Parliament was generally called the 'Bribery Parliament'.[147] Middle class Parliamentary reformers considered that the extension of the franchise would make bribery difficult and intimidation would disappear.[148]

Calls for the extension of the franchise came from an increasingly dissatisfied working class. The Chartist movement had called for male universal suffrage as one of its demands. However until 1852 all government administrations, whether Whig or Tory, had suppressed any effort to reform the Parliamentary franchise.[149]

Lord John Russell, who had been one of the architects of the Great Reform Bills of 30 years before, introduced three bills between 1852 and 1860. All were based on extending the franchise by lowering the value of the property needed to qualify to register. A Conservative Bill in 1859 was to extend the franchise by means of so-called "fancy franchises". These included qualifications such as having bank savings at a certain level, income from certain dividends or being a graduate or in the armed forces or civil service.[150]

Prime Minister Gladstone introduced a Bill in 1866 which would have reduced the value of property required in the boroughs to £7. It would also have removed the requirement that all rates and taxes had to be paid by the occupier, as many borough occupiers had been disfranchised because they had not paid their rates on time or they were paid by their landlord. In the counties the £50 tenant qualification was to be reduced to £14. In both counties and boroughs anyone with savings of £50 deposited in a bank was to be enfranchised. The Bill failed and the Cabinet resigned.[151]

The Bill that followed in 1867, introduced by Disraeli, was a mixture of reducing the value of property required to register and "fancy franchises".[152] Some of the measures which did not find their way into the final Act were the extension of the vote to men based on their education or occupation (graduates, ministers of religion, lawyers, medical practitioners and schoolmasters), having bank savings of £50 or having paid 20 shillings in taxes. The original Bill also had a clause granting a second vote in a borough election if someone qualified under both the residential and "fancy franchise" qualifications.[153]

The Act made further alterations to the distribution of seats including the granting of a seat in the House of Commons to the University of London. The existing electorate of the University seats could now vote by proxy following the passing of the *University Elections Act 1861* and London University was also given this option.[154]

Several Parliamentary boroughs were disfranchised for corruption. The people found guilty of giving or receiving bribes in the boroughs of Totnes, Reigate, Great Yarmouth and Lancaster, were disqualified from voting in subsequent county elections (Sections 12-16 of the RPA 1867).

In seats represented by 3 MPs, those boroughs granted an additional seat by this Act and some counties that were made 3 seat counties in 1832, voters were restricted to two votes (Section 9). Until now in contested elections with three seats a voter could cast three votes. And in the City of London, which still had four seats, the maximum number of votes for each voter was 3 (Section 10).

Borough Franchise

The provisions for the Parliamentary franchise which were finally passed had most impact in the Parliamentary boroughs. The borough franchise was extended to all householders in a house rated for the poor rate and not in receipt of poor relief themselves. Lodgers occupying lodgings worth £10 were also enfranchised.

This measure extended the vote to many working class men, although the lodger franchise was an insignificant part of this; a working class lodger could only register to vote during office hours and would not have wanted to lose wages in order to gain a vote.[155] As a result the borough franchise probably more than doubled. Estimates vary but in England and Wales the borough vote probably rose from about 514,000 (1866) to 1,225,000 (1868).[156] Boroughs which did not return MPs remained subject to the county franchise.

County Franchise

The alteration to the county vote was less significant. The property qualifications were retained with modifications to the qualifying values of copy and leaseholder but no change to the 40 shilling freeholders. The copyholder and leaseholder property values were reduced from £10 to £5. These changes only accounted for about 20% of new registrations.

The most significant change was to the tenant franchise. Occupiers who rented a property of at least £12 (down from £50) could register. This accounted for about 80% of new registrations to the county vote.[157] Across England and Wales the number of county voters went up from about 543,000 (1866) to 791,000 (1868).[158]

Disqualifications

Section 40 of the Act extended the prohibition of men in receipt of poor relief being disqualified from registering to vote to county voters.

Section 11 of the Act prohibited anyone who received payment from a candidate in the six months before an election for the purposes of electioneering (as an agent, canvasser, clerk or messenger or similar role) from voting.

Main changes of the 1867 Reform Act

Borough franchise extended to all male householders as long as the householder was not in receipt of poor relief and met registration requirements. Lodgers occupying lodgings worth £10 also enfranchised.

County franchise thresholds at which men could qualify to register were reduced (for copyholders and leaseholders the qualifying value of the property was reduced to £5 and for tenants the value was reduced to £12).

> Disqualification from registering to vote if in receipt of poor relief was extended to county voters.
>
> Anyone receiving payment from Parliamentary candidates for the purposes of electioneering prevented from voting.
>
> Further reform of the number of seats from Parliamentary boroughs and county divisions.

8. 1868 REFORM ACTS IN SCOTLAND AND IRELAND

The legislation affecting Scotland and Ireland was passed the year after the Second Reform Act. Like the legislation for England and Wales the passage of the legislation was never straight forward and some of the underlying motives for reform were considered to be highly partisan by some commentators.

Scottish and Irish Bills were both promised by Disraeli in March 1867. A Scottish Bill was forthcoming but an Irish Bill was initially delayed and then postponed indefinitely, with Disraeli blaming the political situation in Ireland. He had also had a meeting with influential Irish supporters who had demanded the Irish Bill be dropped in order to secure their support for the English reforms.[159]

A Scottish Reform Bill was introduced first in May 1867 but had to be withdrawn after Scottish Liberals were unhappy that the limited redistribution of seats favoured the Tory counties and Irish MPs of both parties were angry at a suggestion that Scotland's seven extra seats would be at the expense of Irish seats.[160]

A new Bill for Scotland was introduced in 1868 which, while altering the redistribution (English boroughs lost out instead of Irish seats to ensure the House of Commons was not enlarged), was similar in nature.

An Irish Reform Bill was finally introduced with the Scottish Bill in 1868. It had initially attempted redistribution as well as reform of the Parliamentary franchise but the redistribution of seats was thrown out in the face of opposition from the Liberals.[161]

8.1. Scotland

The burgh vote was extended to householders not in receipt of poor relief, and to lodgers in a lodging valued at least £10. The effect on the size of the electorate varied. In Edinburgh the electorate doubled from about 10,000 in 1865 to 21,000 in 1868. In Glasgow it nearly trebled from 16,800 to 47,900.[162] The electorate of the Kilmarnock district of burghs (which comprised 5 burghs in total) increased from 1,645 to 6,531.[163] Across the whole of Scotland the burgh franchise rose from about 55,500 to 152,000.[164]

The county franchise was extended, as in England, by reducing the qualifying thresholds. Free and leasehold owners were allowed to register if their property was valued at £5 and above and tenant occupiers who were in properties of £14 and above provided they had not claimed poor relief were also allowed to register.[165] This extended the county franchise from 50,000 to 75,000.[166]

Men who engaged in paid work on behalf of a candidate at a Parliamentary election, either as agent, canvasser, clerk or messenger, within the six months before an election were barred from voting.[167]

The provisions for the redistribution of seats were modest. An extra MP was granted to each of the Parliamentary boroughs of Glasgow and Dundee and the counties of Lanark, Ayr and Aberdeenshire. Hawick, Galashiels and Selkirk were formed into a new district of burghs seat and the counties of Selkirk and Peebles were merged. In the Glasgow seat voters could cast only two votes to elect the three MPs.

The Act also created university seats for Scotland for the first time. There were to be two seats, with one returned jointly for Edinburgh University and St Andrews University, and the other to represent the Universities of Glasgow and Aberdeen. The electorate was comprised of the Chancellor, members of the University Court, professors and graduates of the four universities. The voters were given the same right to vote by proxy as in university elections in England.

8.2. Ireland

The Irish Reform Act contained no measures for redistribution. The Bill had contained provisions for disfranchising six boroughs, granting an extra seat to Dublin and to alter some of the county seats,[168] but all these measures were dropped following opposition by the Liberals.[169]

The Act reformed the Parliamentary borough franchise by halving the qualifying rateable value of a property from the £8 level, agreed in 1850, to £4.[170] Lodgers in lodgings valued at £10 or above could register to vote.

The county franchise remained at £12 but the Act made provision for joint occupancy registration.

As with Scotland, men who engaged in paid work on behalf of a candidate at a Parliamentary election, either as agent, canvasser, clerk or messenger, within the six months before an election were barred from voting.[171]

According to FB Smith in *The Making of the Second Reform Act*, the "planned increase in voters was negligible, only 9,000, and once Members threw out the redistribution, they hurriedly passed the rest in two nights in a hot sultry June" as a Dissolution of Parliament was imminent. The Scottish and Irish reform Acts were carried "with a minimum of interested, informed discussion and a maximum of irresponsible contempt."[172]

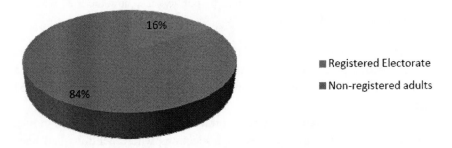

Proportion of adults (21 years +) in Great Britain and Ireland registered to vote 1868.

9. THE BALLOT ACT 1872

The *Parliamentary and Municipal Elections Act 1872,* known as the Ballot Act, did not extend the Parliamentary franchise but altered significantly the way men exercised their vote. Until this Act voting in elections took place by way of a public show of hands or by a public declaration. As noted above, intimidation and bribery to gain votes were commonplace and the requirement to publicly declare your vote did nothing to prevent this.

Attempts had been made to introduce voting by secret ballot in the unsuccessful Reform Bill of 1831. Lord Durham, who drafted the Reform Bill with Lord Russell, had included a provision for a secret ballot in the original draft but this was deleted by Lord Grey, the Prime Minister, in Cabinet, along with provisions for five-year Parliaments.[173]

In the period between the First and Second Reform Acts the Chartist movement had demanded secret voting at Parliamentary elections as a fundamental principle and Radicals in Parliament had introduced various motions in the House of Commons in an attempt to initiate voting by secret ballot.

In 1862 leave was given to introduce a Ballot Bill, with the motion agreed by 83 votes to 50.[174] In the brief Second Reading debate on the Bill, which was defeated (211 votes to 126), the then Home Secretary, Sir George Grey, stated:

> Instead of being a check on bribery, it would facilitate it by preventing detection in many cases...In his opinion, the elective franchise was both a trust and a duty; and, without affirming that the electors were trustees for the whole community, he would say that they ought to be subject to the ordinary rule of letting the public know how the trust was fulfilled and the duty was discharged.[175]

In 1870 a Select Committee of the House of Commons investigated the mode of election at municipal and Parliamentary elections. This was in part a response to the levels of corruption and intimidation that prevailed at the 1868 general election.[176]

The Committee noted that bribery and treating had frequently been proved in many disputed Parliamentary borough elections where petitions had been presented to election courts. It noted that intimidation was harder to prove but was clearly practiced. In county elections fewer petitions and less corruption were apparent but "intimidation and undue influence are very largely practised".[177] On municipal elections it was more scathing, stating that many voters would not vote unless paid, sometimes in drink tickets rather than cash, and rioting often took place on polling day.[178]

The Committee recommended that the secret ballot, the closing of public houses on polling days and the banning of using pub rooms as election committee rooms would "not only promote the tranquility of both municipal and Parliamentary election, but would also protect voters from undue influence and intimidation".[179] The Committee had also noted the extensive deployment of army troops during Irish elections. It considered that this hindered free elections and considered the ballot as the only way of ending a significant military presence in Ireland during elections.[180]

A Bill was introduced and passed by the Commons in 1871 but was thrown out by the House of Lords. The Bill was introduced in the next session but the measure was passed with little enthusiasm and "in spite of the all but unanimous hostility of the House of Lords, the secret disapproval of the House of Commons and the indifference of the general community".[181]

The Ballot Act abolished the open method of voting and introduced the right to vote by secret ballot whereby no one except the voter need know how he voted. The Ballot Act is no longer in force but the historic principle of a secret ballot was carried forward in consolidating legislation.

Little has changed in the process of voting at polling stations since the passing of the Act, which stated:

> In the case of a poll at an election the votes shall be given by ballot. The ballot of each voter shall consist of a paper (in this Act called a ballot paper) showing the names and description of the candidates. Each ballot paper shall have a number printed on the back, and shall have attached a counterfoil with the same number printed on the face. At the time of voting, the ballot paper shall be marked on both sides with an official mark, and delivered to the voter within the polling station, and the number of such voter on the register of voters shall be marked on the counterfoil, and the voter, having secretly marked his vote on the paper, and folded it up so as to conceal his vote, shall place it in a closed box in the presence of the officer presiding at the polling station (in this Act called the 'presiding officer') after having shown to him the official mark at the back.[182]

As a result of the Act, intimidation of voters was undermined although there continued to be instances of corruption. In Worcester, in 1906, there were 500 voters mainly of the "needy and loafing classes" who were prepared to sell their votes for drink or money.[183]

Other attempts were made to tackle the problem of bribery. The *Corrupt Practices Act 1854* was the beginning of regulation of election expenses but the Act was fairly ineffective. Until 1868 Parliament had itself dealt with petitions on disputed elections. House of Commons committees investigated and ruled on accusations of intimidation, corruption, bribery, treating or malpractice at elections.

In 1868 Disraeli succeeding in transferring the consideration of election petitions to the courts, which were less lenient, with further changes to the petition process in 1879. These helped but corruption was not entirely eliminated.[184]

Following the 1880 general election there were 42 election petitions presented. Of these 28 came to trial and for 8 boroughs Royal Commissions were established to investigate in detail bribery during the election.

The judgements of the petitions led the Liberal government to introduce legislation without waiting for the inquiries of the Royal Commissions. [185] The legislation eventually became the *Corrupt and Illegal Practices Act 1883,* which tightened the regulation.[186] Together the *Ballot Act* and the *Corrupt and Illegal Practices Act* formed the basis of modern electoral administration law.[187]

10. THE THIRD REFORM ACT

The *Representation of the People Act 1884,* also known as the Third Reform Act, was the next milestone in the extension of the franchise.[188] It was significant for introducing the first uniform Parliamentary franchise across the whole of Britain and Ireland although it retained almost all of the ancient voting rights still in force at the time the Bill was introduced.

The Reform Act did not include redistribution of seats. Redistribution came as a result of the *Redistribution of Seats Bill.* A Boundary Commission was established to recommend boundaries while the Bill was still going through Parliament. The Commission was appointed in November 1884 and reported in February 1885.[189] The recommendations were incorporated into the Bill which became the *Redistribution of Seats Act 1885.*[190]

The *Redistribution of Seats Act* reformed all county constituencies so that each seat only returned a single MP. Larger towns and cities were divided into single Member borough constituencies but a number of undivided borough seats continued to return 2 MPs (the last two Member seats were abolished in 1950).

The main effect of the Reform Act was to extend the householder voting rights enjoyed in the Parliamentary boroughs to those living in the counties. The Prime Minister, Gladstone, sought leave to introduce the Bill by saying:

> The principle upon which it proceeds is, that the head of every household, under the conditions of the law, shall vote...It is, in point of fact, if it is to be described by a single phrase, a Household Franchise Bill for the United Kingdom".[191]

One reason for the push to equalise the Parliamentary franchise between the Parliamentary boroughs and the counties was the growth of suburban areas. Any boundary alterations that had been implemented in borough seats in 1832 and 1868 had, in most cases, been very modest. With the growth of towns in the Victorian era this had led to many suburban households of the same or similar nature to those within the boundaries of the Parliamentary boroughs being excluded from the Parliamentary franchise. This was because they were beyond the borough boundaries and subject, therefore, to the county franchise.

Another consequence of urban growth was that working men who had been granted borough franchises in 1868 were disfranchised by the need to move beyond the boundaries of the Parliamentary borough to where their work was located. Gladstone highlighted this using Glasgow as his example;

> It is that of the ship-building works on the Clyde. Those works were within the precincts of the City of Glasgow, and the persons who laboured in them were able to remain within the city, being near their work, and at the same time to enjoy the franchise. But the marvellous enterprise of Glasgow, which has made that city the centre and crown of the shipbuilding business of the world, could not be confined within the limits of the City of Glasgow, and it moved down the river. As the trade moved down the river the artisans required to move down the river with it. That was a matter of necessity, and the obedience to that necessity involves, under the present law, wholesale disfranchisement.[192]

Section 2 of the Act stated that "a uniform household franchise and a uniform lodger franchise at elections shall be established in all counties and boroughs throughout the United Kingdom".[193] The Section still explicitly prohibited female enfranchisement by stating "every man" possessed of the household qualification would be entitled to register to vote.

The number of men added to the electoral register, mainly agricultural and other labourers in county seats who had a settled home, was about 2,000,000. This was an increase of nearly 70% and took the electorate to about 5,000,000.[194]

The Act, like its predecessors, did not strip men in England and Wales of their ancient voting rights. However, by 1885-86 those with ancient voting rights, for example resident freemen in the boroughs or county freeholders, numbered only 35,066.[195]

The Act also did not attempt to change plural voting, where men who met the qualification to vote in more than one seat, and were registered to vote in each seat, could continue to do so. This was at a time when general elections took place over many days (voting in a general election on a single day did not start until 1918). In 1910 it was estimated that there were over 500,000 plural votes and at least 80% were affiliated to the Conservative Party.[196] During the Committee stage of the Bill an amendment was tabled to remove plural voting but it was easily defeated.[197]

One form of plural voting that was specifically tackled was the so-called "faggot vote". Attempts had been made to prevent this before but proved unsuccessful (see section 2.1 above) but Section 4 of the 1884 Act specifically restricted the practice. "Faggot votes" were multiple votes derived from one freeholding that conferred an ancient right to the county franchise. If one large freeholding was subdivided into smaller holdings that still each had a value of 40 shillings the subdivision could be granted as a temporary freeholding to other men purely for the purposes of voting.

In the course of the debate on the *Representation of the People Bill 1884* one Member refers to a holding in West Somerset that had been subdivided into 33 separate holdings conferring votes upon "33 Bristol Tory merchants who had nothing to do with West Somerset, and never came there except to vote at the elections".[198]

Section 10 of the 1884 Reform Act contained a provision that any man subject to a legal incapacity to be registered should remain unable to register. By the time of this Act certain statute and common law restrictions had become established (see Section 16 below).

Main changes of the 1884 Reform Act

First uniform Parliamentary franchise across the whole of the United Kingdom (although existing voting rights were retained).

Equalised householder voting qualifications between county and borough franchises partly to take into account the increasing suburban nature of some county seats.

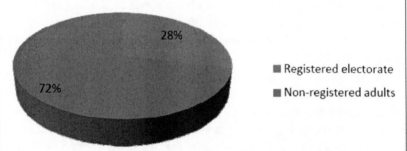

■ Registered electorate

■ Non-registered adults

Source: Robert Blackburn, *The Electoral System in Britain,* 1995, p66.

Proportion of adults (21 years +) registered to vote.

11. FEMALE SUFFRAGE BEFORE 1918

Mary Wollstonecraft is generally recognised as the founder of the movement seeking freedom and equality for women; her book *A Vindication of the Rights of Woman* was published in 1792.[199] As noted above (Section 4) legislation explicitly excluded women from the Parliamentary franchise in 1832,[200] and the first petition presented to Parliament seeking votes at Parliamentary elections was in 1832.[201] It was not until the mid-nineteenth century that the women's suffrage movement gained momentum.

The Second Reform Act in 1867 saw the first serious attempt to debate Parliamentary votes for women.[202] Some women had been allowed to vote in local elections since 1818. The *Vestries Act 1818* allowed women to vote in parish vestry elections although 'this same right was denied married women on the grounds that their husbands would vote on their behalf.'[203]

During the Committee stage of the Second Reform Bill in 1867, one of the MPs for Westminster, John Stuart Mill, introduced an amendment to replace the word 'man' with the word 'person' in order to extend the Parliamentary franchise to women.[204] The amendment was defeated by 196 votes to 73 but women still attempted to register to vote by citing an Act of 1850.[205] This Act stated that words of the masculine gender were to be deemed to refer to females unless expressly noted otherwise. In 1868, a court case in the Court of Common Pleas ruled that the word "man" included women when referring to observance of laws and taxation but included only male persons when referring to the Parliamentary franchise.[206]

Between 1869 and 1884 there were almost annual debates on women's suffrage in Parliament.[207] These were not successful in securing the Parliamentary franchise for women but there was some advancement in local franchises.[208]

In 1869 women in England and Wales were first given the right to vote in local elections. In 1834, when enlarged poor law unions were formed, women parish ratepayers could vote to elect poor law union guardians. However, the *Municipal Corporations Act 1835* denied women this right by defining the local electorate in the same terms as the Great Reform Act, by inserting the words 'male persons'.[209]

The *Municipal Franchise Act 1869* gave the vote and right to stand as poor law guardians to women ratepayers. The right of women to vote and stand for school boards followed in 1870 with the *Elementary Education Act 1870*.[210]

Some married women attempted to register for the local government franchise but a court case in 1872 established that the vote should only be given to single women ratepayers and not the wives and daughters of ratepayers. The courts ruled that the *Municipal Franchise Act 1869* could not override the common law principle that a married woman's rights were subsumed with those of her husband's. Despite this restriction, by 1900 the number of women registered for the local government franchise in England was over 1 million.[211]

In Scotland, 1872 saw women eligible to vote and stand in school board elections and in 1881 women could vote in burgh elections. In England and Wales, the *Local Government Act 1888* gave women ratepayers the vote in borough and county council elections. Votes for women in Scottish county elections followed a year later.[212]

During the passage of the Third Reform Bill, in 1884, an amendment was moved by William Woodall, MP for Stoke-on-Trent, in Committee to extend the Parliamentary franchise to women. On moving his amendment Woodall said:

> No one who has watched the course of public opinion on this subject will hesitate to say that there has been a remarkable and very strong growth of public opinion in its favour. The time has long since gone by when the proposal to enfranchise women was received with derision.[213]

After a lengthy debate the amendment was rejected by 271 votes to 135.[214]

Three Bills which became known as the 'Conciliation Bills' were introduced in 1910, 1911 and 1912 by backbench MPs from all parties. These Bills, all unsuccessful, would have enfranchised certain property-owning women and were not supported by all campaigners for women's suffrage.

The Liberal government of Herbert Asquith introduced a Reform Bill in 1912 to consolidate electoral matters by repealing 30 statutes and partially repealing another 47.[215] The government intended to allow for amendments discussing female suffrage at the Committee stage of the Bill in January 1913, but the Speaker of the House ruled that if the amendments had been carried then the Bill would be substantially altered and would need to be withdrawn and reintroduced as a new Bill.[216]

The withdrawal of the Bill led to increased militancy from parts of the suffragette movement. The subsequent introduction of the *Women's Suffrage Bill* of 1913, a Private Members' Bill facilitated by the government, meant that the issue was dominated by the violence of militant suffragettes rather than the merits of women's suffrage and the Bill was defeated on Second Reading by 269 votes to 221.[217]

At the outbreak of the First World War saw the leading militant organisation campaigning for women's suffrage, the Women's Social and Political Union, led by Emmeline and Christabel Pankhurst, suspend militant action almost immediately and its national organisation was wound up.

The leading peaceful campaigning organisation, the National Union of Women's Suffrage Societies, led by Millicent Fawcett, also mainly re-directed its active work towards the war effort, while campaigning continued behind the scenes. Other smaller organisations attempted to continue campaigning but were hampered by lack of funds and shortages of paper to publish campaign material.[218]

Some women over 30 years of age were first granted the Parliamentary franchise following the *Representation of the People Act 1918* (see below for more detail). The timing of the Act has meant many commentators have concluded that the extension of the Parliamentary franchise to some women was a 'reward' for the patriotism showed by women during the First World War. Others have pointed to the fact that the process that led to the Act was driven more by the need to deal with the disenfranchisement of soldiers and that many of the younger women who contributed most to the munitions work and auxiliary forces remained without the vote.[219] Even those women over 30 were not automatically granted the Parliamentary franchise, their qualification was dependent on qualification to a local government vote, which left 22% of women over 30 disenfranchised.[220]

Overall the War gave both politicians and campaigners the opportunity to change their minds and their tactics, but other reasons were also important including the groundwork done by campaigning organisations before the War, a desire on both sides not to return to militant suffragette action, and a more general change in social attitudes.

12. THE REPRESENTATION OF THE PEOPLE ACT 1918

The Representation of the People Act 1918 was a milestone piece of legislation which created almost universal male suffrage and for the first time allowed some women to vote at Parliamentary elections.

There were no significant changes made to Parliamentary election law between the *Representation of the People Act 1884* (and the *Redistribution of Seats Act 1885* which was an accompanying piece of legislation following on from extending the Parliamentary franchise) and the *Representation of the People Act 1918.*[221]

There had been several attempts to alter aspects of electoral law but it had been difficult to find common ground.

Various attempts had been made to enfranchise women and the issues of plural voting, universal male suffrage and electoral registration had all been raised in Parliament in the early years of the twentieth century.

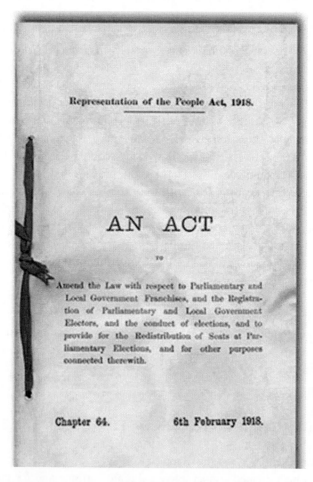

Representation of the People Act 1918, Parliamentary Archives, HL/PO/PU/1/1918/7&8G5c64 © Parliamentary copyright images are reproduced with the permission of Parliament.

Asquith's Reform Bill in 1912 attempted to consolidate electoral matters by repealing 30 statutes and partially repealing another 47.[222]

There was little cross party support for the main electoral issues and the Bill failed. Women's suffrage was generally opposed by Conservatives MPs and supported by Liberal MPs.[223] However, a number of Liberal cabinet members, including Asquith, personally opposed giving women the vote, and others including Lloyd George opposed giving the vote only to propertied women, which would benefit the Conservatives. Attempts to abolish plural voting were also opposed by the Conservatives.[224] The First World War brought about a political truce between the parties and also between politicians and suffragettes.

The Parliamentary electoral register in force at the outbreak of the First World War continued but all local elections were postponed and registration ceased in July 1915. In January 1916 the *Parliament and Registration Act 1916* made provision for the extension of Parliament (the Parliament would have had to been dissolved at the beginning of February had no provision been made to extend its life).

There was little demand for a general election but the wartime coalition was initially fragile and a general election continued to be a real possibility.[225] This focused attention on electoral registration. The electoral register was becoming increasingly out of date and if a new register was to be prepared only about 50% of electors would be able to register because of war work taking them away from their homes. Many soldiers would be also disenfranchised because they were absent from home.[226]

Prime Minister Asquith announced that the Coalition Government had been unable to agree on a solution and a select committee of the House would be formed to examine the issue. The motion was tabled on 19 July 1916 but it was not received well by the House of Commons as many Members felt the important issues should be settled by the government and not a Select Committee which had no power to make its decisions binding.[227] Asquith closed the debate, having appeared in the Commons Chamber after being told how the debate was going, by withdrawing the motion:

> The Government, after most carefully considering the matter in all its aspects and finding it exceedingly difficult to arrive at a practical solution, thought this was a matter concerning primarily the House of Commons, and they thought that the assistance and advice of a Select Committee might constitutionally be invoked. If the House does not think so I certainly shall not press the Motion.[228]

The problem for the government was how best to deal with the problems of registration without raising fundamental questions about the Parliamentary franchise and eligibility to register. If questions of the franchise were raised the controversial question of votes for women would inevitably have to be included. The government also faced pressure to deal with registration before the end of the life of the Parliament or face opposition to further extend the life of the Parliament.[229]

In the end the government extended the life of the Parliament with the *Parliament and Local Election Act 1916* and introduced a separate Bill to deal with registration, the *Special Register Bill 1916.* The Bill attempted to temporarily solve the problems of war time registration without dealing with the registration and enfranchisement of soldiers, who would have been disenfranchised by their absence from a qualifying household. Just before the Second Reading stage of the Bill the Speaker ruled that any amendment to enfranchise soldiers or women tabled to the Committee stage would render the Bill a new Bill.[230] The Bill was later dropped.[231]

During the Second Reading debate Walter Long, MP for the Strand division of Westminster and President of the Board of Local Government, who had introduced the Bill, said:

> I myself believe that if we agreed amongst ourselves, and the Government offered any assistance which they could, and which, I believe, they would gladly do, to set up—I will not say a Committee, because that is not exactly what I mean— but a representative conference, not only of parties, but of groups, a conference which would really represent opinion on these three subjects: electoral reform, revision of your electoral power when you have got it, and registration, I believe— and I do not speak altogether out of books—that such a conference of earnest men, holding strong views, bitterly opposed to each other, if they were face to face with these difficulties...would produce an agreed system for all three questions upon which the great mass of opinion of the people of this country could come together.[232]

This idea led to the creation of the Speaker's Conference that eventually gave rise to the *Representation of the People Act 1918.*[233]

The conference was established in October 1916 under the chairmanship of the Speaker, James Lowther, although he accepted the position without enthusiasm.[234] It was designed to represent a broad range of opinions. There were 5 Members of the House of Lords (3 Conservative/Unionist and 2

Liberals) and 27 Members of the House of Commons (11 Conservative/Unionist, 10 Liberals, 3 Nationalists and 3 Labour).

The members of the conference were fairly evenly split between supporters and opponents of women's suffrage and also between universal male suffrage and those that favoured the status quo.[235] The Conference was not a formally constituted Committee of the House and there was no precedent to limit its options.[236]

The Conference reported its findings by way of a letter from the Speaker to the Prime Minister, by this time David Lloyd-George.[237] Agreement had been found in all the areas it had been asked to inquire into: the reform of the franchise, redistribution of Parliamentary seats, reform of electoral registration and the method of costs of elections.

Most of the suggested measures were agreed unanimously (including the use of the single transferable vote in multi-Member constituencies, redistribution of seats, retaining university seats and electoral registration). However, the granting of female suffrage, allowing postal voting, not disqualifying someone from registering to vote if they had claimed poor relief and the use of the alternative vote in single Member constituencies were agreed by majority.

The two most controversial measures in the Bill,[238] proportional representation in multi-Member seats and women's suffrage, were included on the understanding that free votes would take place in the House of Commons on whether they were to be retained in the Bill; the government would accept the decision of the House.

The two most significant effects of the Act were to introduce near-universal male suffrage and to extend the Parliamentary franchise to some women for the first time. The provisions were in separate parts of the Act and the qualifications for men and women were quite different.

12.1. Male Suffrage

On the recommendations of the Speaker's Conference the new Act swept away all previous existing rights to the Parliamentary franchise (with the exception of a provision for Liverymen in the City of London). The Act repealed 31 existing statutes dealing with the franchise and registration and part-repealed 32 more.[239]

In order to register for Parliamentary elections men had to be 21 years, not subject to any legal incapacity to vote and to have satisfied the requisite residence or business premises occupation qualification.

The Bill as introduced included a provision to maintain the restriction that men who had claimed poor relief or alms during the qualifying period were prevented from registering to vote, but this was removed during the passage of the Bill.[240] It therefore meant that there would be near universal suffrage for men aged 21 or over (some restrictions remained, see Section 12 below). It meant that around 13 million men were now eligible to register to vote.[241]

For non-business residence the value of the property, the payment of rates or the freehold/leasehold/tenant status of the voter was no longer relevant. Temporary absence from the residence during the qualifying 6 months no longer stripped a voter of the right to register. Men who lived in educational or religious institutions, police barracks and male domestic servants could all now register.[242] It also permitted sons who were of age but still living at home to register.[243] Men who had a business premises valued at £10 which they had occupied for six months could register for a business vote.

Unrestricted plural voting was prohibited but dual voting was allowed, although a second vote could only be cast if the qualifying business premises was in a separate constituency to the residence premises.[244]

For both residence and business franchises a man could still register if he had moved within the six months qualifying period as long as he had moved within the Parliamentary borough or county or to a neighbouring constituency. Neighbouring constituencies could be across water as long as the stretch of water was not more than six miles wide, such as on Clydeside.[245]

The university Parliamentary franchise was granted to all male graduates who were of age and who were graduates of one of the universities that formed one of the university constituencies. There were two seats each for Oxford and Cambridge. The Universities of London and Wales got one seat each and there were two seats for a combined university constituency comprising the universities of Durham, Manchester (Victoria University) Liverpool, Leeds, Sheffield, Birmingham and Bristol. A combined Scottish universities seat returned three MPs and comprised the universities of St Andrews, Glasgow, Aberdeen and Edinburgh.[246] The universities constituencies which returned more than one Member used the single transferable vote system to elect the Members. The 1918 Act also revised and simplified the local government franchise for men. A uniform local government franchise was granted to all men in occupation of land or premises whether they were owner or tenant as long as they had been there for the qualifying period.

Main effects of the Representation of the People Act 1918

Universal male suffrage. All previous ancient and nineteenth century voting rights were repealed and all men over the age of 21 were able to register to vote in Parliamentary elections as long as they fulfilled residence requirements and were not legally disqualified from registering to vote.

First female suffrage. Women over 30 could register for a Parliamentary vote as long as they (or their husband) qualified for a local government vote. The Act also gave single women over 21 the local government franchise.

Absent voting for military personnel. This included women but the 30 year old restriction still applied. Men in the military could register and vote from 19 years of age.

Those in receipt of poor relief or alms no longer prohibited from registering to vote.

First Act to codify that only British subjects could register to vote in Parliamentary elections (this had previously been a common law restriction).

Conscientious objectors prevented from registering to vote until 5 years after the conclusion of the Great War.

University seat electorates extended to all male graduates who were of age and graduates of those universities that returned MPs or formed part of the combined universities seats.

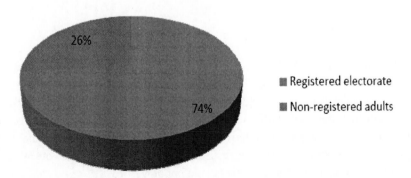

Source: Robert Blackburn, *The Electoral System in Britain,* 1995, p66.

Proportion of adults (21+) registered to vote.

The meaning of tenant was applied to lodgers of unfurnished rooms and also those residing in an employer's premises in which the employer did not reside (lodgers in furnished rooms were excluded).

This meant that people like school masters or shop assistants who occupied separate living quarters within a business premises could register for the local government franchise for the first time (they had been able to register as Parliamentary voters since 1884).[247]

12.2. Female Suffrage

The vote on retaining the clause on women's suffrage in the Bill was passed by 385 votes to 55.[248] Debate then followed on the exact terms of women's suffrage. Equality with men was never seriously considered as it would have enfranchised up to 14,000,000 women and would have outnumbered the number of men able to register.[249]

Women were allowed to register as Parliamentary voters if they were 30 years old and qualified for a local government franchise. The local government franchise for women was also altered by the 1918 Act (it was extended to all single women over the age of 21 on the same basis as men and in a residence where a husband and wife resided the woman could qualify for the local government franchise if she was 30 years or older).

As a result of the Act 8.4 million women were granted the Parliamentary franchise.[250]

12.3. Armed Forces Voting

Special provisions were made for those serving in the Great War. A person serving in His Majesty's forces or in certain other roles which meant they were away from home and would therefore lose the right to a residence vote could register as a Parliamentary elector. It excluded munitions workers which meant many who had moved to munitions factories were unable to register. Those personnel serving in Belgium and France could vote by post and other absent armed forces voters could appoint a proxy.[251]

The Armed Forces voting provisions had originally related to the Great War and were due to expire twelve months after the end of the War.[252] In the Act as passed, there was no time limit and the provisions applied permanently during peace time.[253]

Men and women were covered by the provisions but as with the general franchise provisions women had to be 30 years old. Men in the Armed Forces covered by these provisions could register and vote from the age of 19 years.[254]

13. UNIVERSAL ADULT SUFFRAGE

The *Representation of the People (Equal Franchise) Act 1928* was the measure that led to an equal and universal adult franchise for elections in the United Kingdom. Prime Minister Stanley Baldwin confirmed the Government had invited the Speaker to preside over another conference similar to that of 1916-17 but that the Speaker had declined to preside because redistribution of seats and electoral matters had become highly partisan.[255] Instead the Government introduced a Bill to deal with the single issue of equal franchise as "question of giving women the vote on the same terms as men there was no difference amongst the parties".[256]

Equal franchise had been a continuing issue for women's campaigning organisations ever since 1918. The House of Commons passed a bill in favour of equal franchise as early as 1919, and equal franchise bills were presented to Parliament every year from 1919 onwards. However many Conservative MPs feared what became known in sections of the popular press as 'the flapper vote', and some argued strongly that equal franchise should be given at age 25, rather than age 21. Winston Churchill was one of the strongest opponents of equal franchise in the Cabinet. It was not until 1927, following the report of a Cabinet Committee and with strong personal support from Baldwin and William Joynson-Hicks, that the Cabinet reached agreement on votes for women at age 21 without a Speaker's Conference.[257]

The Home Secretary, Sir William Joynson-Hicks, opened the Second Reading debate on the Bill and explained the affect the provisions would have on the number of registered voters:

> We have, in round figures, 12,250,000 men and 9,250,000 women, leaving men with a majority of something over 3,000,000. When this Bill is passed, the majority will be 2,000,000 the other way, that is, 2,000,000 more women than men with the vote. But if we accept the principle of establishing representation in this country on the broadest possible basis...then we cannot possibly leave more than 5,000,000 [women] over the age of 21 unrepresented by their votes in this House of Commons.[258]

The Bill received its Second Reading in the House of Commons on 29 March 1928 and was passed by 387 votes to 10.[259]

Section 1 of the Act repealed the sections of the 1918 RPA that dealt with the different franchises for men and women and substituted two new sections that dealt with the Parliamentary franchise and the local government franchise. Both new sections stated that a "person shall be entitled" to register to vote and therefore assimilated the franchises of men and women to make them equal regardless of sex as long as the person was not subject to any legal incapacity to vote.

Section 1 also equalised the university Parliamentary franchise by removing the 30 year old age limit on female graduates from relevant universities voting in the university seats. Section 2 of the Act equalised the local government franchise for men and women

The Act also re-enacted the provision that restricted those entitled to register for three votes (residence, business and university) to one residence vote (regardless of in how many constituencies the person qualified for a residence vote) and to use only one other vote. The person could choose whether to vote for a university seat or for a constituency where they qualified for a business vote but not use both (Section 4).

14. THE REPRESENTATION OF THE PEOPLE ACT 1948

The next landmark in the evolution of the Parliamentary franchise came with the *Representation of the People Act 1948*. It followed a Speaker's conference established in 1944 to consider electoral reform and the redistribution of seats.[260]

This was the last Act to deal with redistribution of seats, the franchise and conduct of elections in a single Act. The Act repealed the 1918 RPA and the *Representation of the People (Equal Franchise) Act 1928*, amongst others, and re-enacted the main provisions relating to the franchise, conduct of elections, and absent voting for service voters and others prevented from voting in person (e.g., police officers involved on duty or those involved with the conduct of the poll).

The Parliamentary franchise remained unaltered with all British resident subjects aged 21 years and over able to register to vote as long as they were not legally incapacitated from doing so. The local government franchise was the same with the exception that the legal incapacity to vote at local government elections was not exactly the same; Peers in Parliament could vote at local government elections. The local government franchise continued to allow business premises holders to register to vote (Section 21(a)(ii)) but the Act abolished the business vote for the Parliamentary franchise.

Section 1 (2) of the Act explicitly stated that a registered voter could only vote in one constituency. Section one also stated that every Parliamentary constituency in the country should return a single Member of Parliament. This abolished the last of the multi-Member seats and the Act also abolished university constituencies by virtue of their omission from the Schedule that defined the constituencies in the UK. It meant for the first time that each Parliamentary elector was entitled to a single vote.

The RPA 1948 re-enacted many of the existing provisions relating to registration of voters and conduct of elections but for the first time the two separate electoral registers, those for the Parliamentary franchise and for the local government franchise, were combined. Section 23 (2) of the Act stated:

> The two registers shall so far as practicable be combined, the names of persons registered only as local government electors being marked to indicate that fact.

15. THE REPRESENTATION OF THE PEOPLE ACT 1969

The next major change to the Parliamentary franchise, like those of 1918 and 1948, followed a Speaker's Conference. The Conference was established in 1965 to consider the minimum voting age; methods and conduct of election; election expenses generally; the use of broadcasting at elections and the cost of election petitions.[261] It reported in 1968 and made 71 recommendations, 60 of which were accepted by the Government. The resulting Bill also included provisions relating to local government elections from a similar conference on local government election law.[262]

The Speaker's conference recommended lowering the age at which people could vote to 20 but the Government introduced the *Representation of the People Bill* with a provision to reduce the voting age to 18.

As the Bill was going through Parliament the *Family Law Reform Bill* was also being considered. One of the main provisions in that Bill was that the age of majority in terms of the law was reduced from 21 to 18 years of age. Schedule 2 of the *Family Law Reform Act 1949* as passed, specifically exempted Representation of the People Acts from being affected by this change and therefore the *Family Law Reform Act* had no bearing on the age at which people could vote.

On the Second Reading of the *Representation of the People Bill* the Home Secretary, James Callaghan, spoke on the Government's decision to opt for a reduction of the voting age to 18:

> Clause 1 is a major part of the Bill. It reduces the minimum age for voting at Parliamentary and local government elections to 18. It is clear, from our earlier debates and from the recommendations of your conference, Mr. Speaker, that there is general agreement that some reduction in the age is called for. As I see it, the choice lies between the age of 20, which was recommended by Mr. Speaker's Conference, and the age of 18, which was the age of majority recommended by the Latey Committee for other than civic purposes and which is now embodied in the Family Law Reform Bill, which, I understand, will be considered in another place next week. The arguments were fully gone into in the debate on the White Paper, and the Government have considered the matter again in the light of that debate.
>
> A number of hon. Members, and especially those who served on your conference, Mr. Speaker, put the case for fixing the age at 20. Others, including those who did not serve on that conference, thought that the age would be better at 18. Sufficient spoke in favour of 18 to give a fair indication that the sense of the House is divided on this matter. [HON. MEMBERS: "Hear, hear."] That would not be unusual in a Chamber of this sort. There is, I think, little need for me today, having gone into the age question only a month ago, to repeat all the arguments I adduced then. There is no new argument of which I am aware.
>
> Eighteen is the age which Latey found to be suitable for the assumption of civic responsibilities. It is an age which appeals to the Government as being appropriate for the casting of a vote. This is a matter of judgment and opinion on which the House will want to make up its mind, the Government having made up their mind, as I have indicated.[263]

An amendment was tabled during the Committee stage of the *Representation of the People Bill* to substitute the age of 18 with the age of 20 recommended by the Speaker's Conference. The Home Secretary reiterated the Government's opposition to the voting age being 20 years:

> I sum up what I have said. It will become increasingly difficult to explain to young people why for all social purposes they are entitled to regard themselves as adult at the age of 18, except on the question of the

vote. I believe that this would be an anomaly that would become increasingly difficult to explain.[264]

The Amendment was rejected 275 votes to 121.[265]

16. DISQUALIFICATIONS FROM VOTING

The RPAs of 1884 and 1918 and subsequent legislation has granted the Parliamentary franchise to those that satisfied the criteria set out in each piece of legislation as long as they were not "subject to any legal incapacity" to register.

Some of the restrictions were as a result of common law and some were included in the legislation. The main disqualifications related to Members of the House of Lords, prisoners, foreigners and the mentally ill. Below is a brief overview of main disqualifications that exist or have existed in the past.

16.1. Peers

Peers sitting in the House of Lords have long been subject to a common law prohibition from registering to vote in Parliamentary elections.[266] The House of Commons explicitly resolved in 1699 that no Peer of the Kingdom had "any right to give his vote in the election" of a Member of the House of Commons by way of a sessional order. The order was modified over the years in relation to Peers who did not have a seat in the House of Lords, for example Peers of Ireland were exempted from the ban, but the general prohibition remained.[267]

In 1872 two Peers challenged their removal from the electoral register in their respective counties. The Courts ruled that a Peer of Parliament was incapacitated from electing a Member of the House of Commons and could not therefore appear on the register.[268] At that time all peers with seats in the House of Lords were hereditary peers. Following the introduction of Life Peers the prohibition on registering to vote in Parliamentary elections was extended to Life Peers.

Following the removal from the House of Lords of all but 91 hereditary peers (following the *House of Lords Act 1999*) the general common law restriction was replaced by a specific disqualification that only Members of the House of Lords were prevented from registering to vote at Parliamentary elections. It meant that the peers who had lost their membership of the second chamber, and therefore who no longer formed part of the three estates of Parliament (Sovereign, Lords and Commons), were no longer prevented from registering to vote in Parliamentary elections for the House of Commons. [269]

Today the Lords Spiritual, the Archbishops of Canterbury and York and the 24 most senior Bishops of the Church of England, by convention do not vote in House of Commons elections, but whether there is a restriction on them voting in Parliamentary elections has never been tested in the courts. The Lords Spiritual are not Peers of Parliament and sit in the House of Lords in an *ex officio* capacity. In 1983 the Archbishop of Canterbury, Dr Robert Runcie, revealed he had voted at the general election of that year but whether or not his vote was valid was never tested.[270]

16.2. Peeresses in Their Own Right

Section 9 (5) of the RPA 1918 Act extended the Parliamentary franchise to peeresses in their own right (as long as they were 30 years of age). Peers with the right to sit in the House of Lords were unable to vote (see above). Most hereditary peerages were created by letters patent which specified the titles passed to the "heirs male of the body".

Some early English peerages and many Scottish peerages allowed for titles to be passed to daughters in the absence of a son. In these cases the right to sit in the House of Lords associated with the peerage was suspended until they passed back to a male. Hereditary peeresses in their own right were not permitted to take their seats in the House of Lords until 1963, at which point they lost their right to vote in Parliamentary elections.[271]

16.3. Those in Receipt of Poor Relief

The Reform Act of 1832 had prevented men in borough constituencies from registering to vote if they were in receipt of poor relief or alms. This restriction was extended to county voters following the Second Reform Act of 1867.

The *Representation of the People Bill 1917/18* as introduced included a provision to retain the disqualification to register to vote if someone had been in receipt of poor relief or alms but this was removed. The Act as passed explicitly stated that receipt of poor relief or alms no longer disqualified a person from registering for Parliamentary or local government elections (Section 9 (1)).

16.4. Those in the Employ of a Candidate

Since 1867 anyone who received payment from a candidate in the six months before an election for the purposes of electioneering (as an agent, canvasser, clerk or messenger or similar role) from voting (see Section 6).

Section 9 (4) of the RPA 1918 ended the disqualification to vote at Parliamentary or local elections on anyone who was paid by or on behalf of a candidate for the purposes of the election.

16.5. Mental Capacity

Case law dating back to at least the 18th century suggested that persons might be regarded as legally incapable of voting solely by reason of their mental state. The case law referred to such persons as 'idiots' and 'lunatics'.[272] A distinction was made between lunatics, who had periods of lucidity, and idiots who were permanently mentally impaired. This restriction remained in place until 2006.

The *Electoral Administration Act 2006* abolished the common law rule which rendered people unable to vote on the basis of mental incapacity

> 73 Abolition of common law incapacity: mental state
> (1) Any rule of the common law which provides that a person is subject to a legal incapacity to vote by reason of his mental state is abolished.[273]

The measure was added to the Bill at Report Stage in the House of Lords by Lord Rix. [274] He had spoken on the issue at Second Reading stage

> While the language of "mental handicap" may still be clinging to life in some quarters, there are some words which nobody today would use and which everyone would now recognise as offensive, insulting and dehumanising. However, perhaps I should say "everyone except lawyers", because existing case law governing people's legal capacity to vote specifically states that "idiots" cannot vote, while "lunatics" can vote only during their lucid moments. No doubt some archaic pieces of case

law no longer matter enough to be challenged, but this one has important symbolic and practical effects. The symbolic effect is to say to people with learning disabilities and mental health problems that calling them idiots and lunatics is acceptable; if the term is in law, why should not everyone use it? The practical effect is that, even today, it is widely and mistakenly believed that people with a learning disability or mental health problems do not possess that most basic of rights in a democracy—the right to vote and have a say in who represents them and governs the country. [275]

The current Electoral Commission guidance for Electoral Registration Officers states.

> ...persons who meet the other registration qualifications are eligible for registration regardless of their mental capacity or lack thereof. Electoral Registration Officers should therefore ensure that persons with learning difficulties or mental health conditions are included in the register of electors. [276]

16.6. Prisoners

The disenfranchisement of prisoners in Great Britain dates back to the *Forfeiture Act 1870* and was linked to the notion of 'civic death'. The 1870 Act denied offenders their rights of citizenship. [277] This had not always been the case, in Norwich in the eighteenth century the returning officer was permitted to enter the city prison to take the vote of freemen who had been imprisoned. [278]

In a publication relating to the *Representation of the People Act 1918* (see below) J Renwick Seager explained that anyone convicted of a felony who had been sentenced to death or imprisonment for a term exceeding twelve months was unable to register to vote. [279]

Those convicted of corrupt practices at a Parliamentary or local government election were prevented from being registered to vote at elections for seven years. [280]

The restriction on prisoners serving a custodial sentence from being registered to vote continues and is enforced by the *Representation of the People Act 1983* as amended. In October 2005 the European Court of Human Rights ruled that the UK's current ban on all serving prisoners from voting contravened Article 3 of Protocol No 1 of the European Convention on Human

Rights. The UK Government has yet to change the law to comply with the Court's ruling.[281]

16.7. Aliens

Only British citizens were entitled to register as voters. Before the requirement was codified it was regarded in common law that a person had to be a British subject to be entitled to register to vote (as long as the other requirements were satisfied). People born within the British Empire and its Dominions were considered British subjects and therefore had the same status. The *British Nationality and Status of Aliens Act 1914* codified what constituted a British subject and therefore could be used to determine which British (and Empire) subjects were entitled to register to vote in Parliamentary elections.[282]

The RPA 1918 Act explicitly stated that only British subjects could register to vote (Section 9(3)). The Act also made some alterations and additional provisions in relation to disqualifications from registering to vote.

Since 1918 the Empire has been replaced by the Commonwealth. The creation of the Irish Free State and Northern Ireland in 1922 and the subsequent formal separation of Ireland from the United Kingdom led to different electoral arrangements for Commonwealth and Irish citizens. All Irish citizens resident in the United Kingdom and qualifying Commonwealth citizens are eligible to vote in UK Parliamentary elections (see Section 20 for more detail). Citizens of non-Commonwealth countries remain ineligible to register to vote in UK Parliamentary elections.

Citizens of EU countries who are resident in the UK can be registered to vote in local government, devolved legislature and European Parliament elections but they are not able to vote in Westminster Parliamentary elections.

16.8. Conscientious Objectors

A temporary measure was included in the RPA 1918 to disqualify conscientious objectors from registering to vote until five years after the War. This included those court-martialled for conscientious objection. There were exemptions from disqualification if the conscientious objector had undertaken work of national importance, as certified by a tribunal.

17. THE REPRESENTATION OF THE PEOPLE ACT 1983

There had been other minor measures passed between 1969 and 1983 but the RPA 1983 was a consolidation measure and currently forms the primary piece of legislation on electoral law in the UK.

The Bill was introduced in the House of Lords and received its Second Reading on the 2 December 1982. The Lord Chancellor, Lord Hailsham of St Marylebone, introduced the Bill:

> My Lords, I rise to move that this Bill be now read a second time. It is a strict consolidation Bill, bringing together in one Act much of the existing law on elections and electoral procedure. This is the second consolidation of the electoral legislation. The arrangement of the present Bill broadly follows that of the first consolidation, the *Representation of the People Act 1949*. Its contents fall under four main heads: the franchise and registration of electors; the conduct of elections; election campaigns; and legal proceedings following elections. The Bill applies to all parliamentary and local government elections in the United Kingdom, except that the local government provisions do not apply to Northern Ireland. The Bill also provides for the repeal of certain obsolete provisions in the existing legislation.[283]

As the Bill was a consolidation measure it passed all its stages in the House of Commons without debate on the 2 February 1983.[284] The granting of Royal Assent was reported to both Houses on 8 February 1983.[285]

The Act, although subsequently amended on a number of occasions, remains the primary parent Act that forms the basis of electoral law in the UK. The landscape in which the RPA 1983, as amended, operates has significantly altered. Devolution, the use of different voting systems for different elections, the extension of absent voting on demand (see below), changes to election timetables and proposed changes to electoral registration have not led to big changes in eligibility to vote in Parliamentary elections but have required many amendments to existing legislation governing the administration of elections.

In July 2012 the Law Commission published its latest programme of law reform. It included a project to review of electoral law in the UK.[286] Electoral law revision would need to be UK-wide and the Law Commission, in cooperation with the Scottish Law Commission and the Northern Ireland Law Commission, launched a consultation on the scope of the project.[287] In announcing the scoping consultation the Law Commission noted that:

Elections are the principal mechanism by which citizens exercise their rights over those who govern in their name. The law governing the administration of elections should therefore meet the reasonable expectations of citizens, electoral administrators, and other participants.

That cannot necessarily be said of the current legal framework for electoral administration. The current law is spread between some 25 major statutes and many pieces of secondary legislation, with the general approach being very detailed prescriptive rules governing each species of election. This results in the law being overly complex, inaccessible, and voluminous.[288]

The Law Commission has indicated that the formulating and consulting on the substantive proposals in the project would occur between February 2013 and July 2015 with final recommendations expected in early 2017.[289]

18. OVERSEAS VOTERS

During the 1970s there was pressure to extend the Parliamentary franchise to British citizens living and working abroad.[290] Representations were made to the Speaker's Conference on Electoral Law in 1973-4, but the Conference did not make specific recommendations in this area. The Home Affairs Select Committee subsequently recommended in 1982-3 that all UK citizens resident in EEC countries should have the right to vote in British Parliamentary elections.[291]

The Government response to the Committee's report recommended a seven year limit, noting that 'in the Government's view a person's links with the United Kingdom are likely to have weakened significantly if he has lived outside it for as long as ten years'.[292] The Government also recommended that the right be extended to British citizens living in non-EEC countries, noting that it would find it hard to defend provisions giving British citizens the right to vote in Paris, but not in New York.

There was a period of consultation before legislative proposals were brought forward; the *Representation of the People Act 1985* made provision for British citizens who were resident overseas to remain on the electoral register in the UK for a period of 5 years.

The level of overseas registration under the 1985 Act was far lower than expected despite overseas publicity. Some of the apparent lack of enthusiasm for the new scheme was attributable to its practical complications, including the need for the elector to take all the positive steps to register without reminders.

In the Parliamentary session 1988-89 a further Bill was introduced to extend and simplify the scheme. Some of the qualifying aspects, such as requiring attestation by a consular official, were removed. The Bill as introduced proposed a 25 year period, but this was reduced to 20 years following amendments which were accepted by the Government. The Bill was enacted as the *Representation of the People Act 1989.*

The qualifying time limit was further amended by the *Political Parties, Elections and Referendums Act 2000.* Section 141 of the Act reduced the qualifying period to 15 years and the change took effect on 1 April 2002. [293]

In 2009 the Electoral Commission released figures that over 5,000,000 British citizens lived overseas but at that time only 13,000 were registered to vote.[294] Between 1987 and 2011 the peak number of overseas voters registered has never exceeded 35,000.[295]

19. ABSENT VOTING

Absent voting for those in the armed services was established in 1918 (see Section 11 above) and some civilians were allowed to cast an absent vote following the *Representation of the People Act 1948.*[296]

In The RPA 1985, which granted the right to register to vote to some British citizens resident overseas (see above), also extended the right to request an absent vote to anyone who was unable to vote in person on polling day.

Overseas voters could only register to vote in Parliamentary elections but those who were resident in Great Britain (the new provisions did not extend to Northern Ireland) who could apply for postal votes could apply to vote in any election.

Absent voting on demand, regardless of whether you were able to get to your allotted polling station was made possible by the *Representation of the People Act 2000.* The *Representation of the People (England & Wales) Regulations 2001* introduced the changes to the absent voting arrangements from 16 February 2001.[297] It was no longer necessary to state a reason for applying for an absent vote, or to obtain attestation of illness etc. from a medical practitioner or employer. Applications may be requested and allowed for an indefinite period, a definite period, or a particular election.[298]

20. THE PARLIAMENTARY FRANCHISE FOR NON-BRITISH CITIZENS

All Irish citizens resident in the United Kingdom and qualifying Commonwealth citizens resident in the UK are eligible to vote in all UK elections, including Parliamentary elections.

Citizens of all other countries are unable to register to vote in Parliamentary elections unless they become naturalised British subjects.

Citizens of EU countries who are resident in the UK can be registered to vote in local government, devolved legislature and European Parliament elections but they are not able to vote in Westminster Parliamentary elections. Citizens of any other countries who are resident in the UK are not eligible to register to vote in any elections.

20.1. Citizens of the Republic of Ireland

Citizens of the Republic of Ireland who are resident in the UK are eligible to register for to and vote in elections in the UK. This is a result of the historical political ties between the two countries and stems from the fact that Ireland was at one time formally a part of the United Kingdom. The *Act of Settlement 1701,* as well as settling the Protestant Succession to the Crown, also contained a clause (no longer in force) that stated:

> No person born out of the Kingdoms of England, Scotland, or Ireland, or the dominions thereunto belonging (although he be naturalized or made a denizen, except such as are born of English parents) shall be capable to be of the Privy Council, or a member of either House of Parliament, or to enjoy any office or place of trust, either civil or military, or to have any grant of lands, tenements or hereditaments from the Crown, to himself or to any other or others in trust for him

After the establishment of the Irish Free State in 1922 the situation became rather less clear. The position was described in a Home Office memorandum which was submitted to the Home Affairs Select Committee in November 1982:

> When the south of Ireland was constituted as a free state within the Commonwealth in 1922 people from both the north and south of Ireland continued to enjoy the same status of British subject. But the policy of

external association which the Irish government adopted in 1936 made its precise relationship with the Commonwealth uncertain, and Irish citizens were regarded as British subjects throughout the Commonwealth but not in the south of Ireland itself.[299]

The *Representation of the People Act 1948* continued the requirement that only British subjects could register to vote. At the time the complex nature of the relationship between the United Kingdom and the Republic of Ireland gave rise to provisions that allowed Irish citizens to continue to register as if they were British subjects.

The *British Nationality Act 1948* resolved the position by making provision for any citizen of the Republic of Ireland, who would previously been a British subject because of Ireland's former position as part of the United Kingdom, not to cease being considered a British subject. This special status was further confirmed by the *Ireland Act 1949* which was an Act to confirm the constitutional position between the Republic of Ireland and the United Kingdom.

The Act formally recognised that the Republic of Ireland ceased to be part of His Majesty's dominions but Section 1 (2) confirmed that Northern Ireland continued to form of the United Kingdom and would not cease to form part of it "without the consent of the Parliament of Northern Ireland" (Northern Ireland had a devolved Parliament at this time).

Section 2 of the Act explicitly stated that "the Republic of Ireland is not a foreign country for the purposes of any law in force in any part of the United Kingdom or in any colony". It reaffirmed the principle in the *British Nationality Act 1948* that Irish citizens should not be considered aliens.

Clement Attlee, as Prime Minister, set out the rationale for this conclusion at second reading of the *Ireland Act 1949*:

> As everybody knows, there are in Britain large numbers of people of Irish descent, some born in Eire and some born in this country, and there is a continual passage to and fro of people who come over to work or to study or for pleasure. It would be an extremely difficult thing to decide in every case from day to day as to what the exact status was of a person with an Irish name, and if we had had to attempt to make all citizens of Eire aliens, it would have involved a great expenditure of men and money and a great extension of the control of aliens. We had in particular also to remember the difficulties caused because of the fact of the land frontier between Northern Ireland, which is part of the United Kingdom and the Commonwealth, and Eire.

We therefore came to the conclusion that we should reciprocally decide that the people of Eire and the people of Britain should not be foreign to one another. Indeed, I go further. The same action may be taken by other Commonwealth countries. I do not pretend that the solution at which we arrived is completely logical – very few things in the relationship between these islands have been completely logical – but I believe they are practical and I believe that they are to our mutual benefit. I am aware, of course, that hitherto there has been this division in international law – it has come down from the past – in which one has recognised people as either belonging to or foreign, but international law is made for men, not men for international law. We are moving into a time when various other relationships are being created. Therefore we thought this was the most practical solution.[300]

The *British Nationality Act 1981* s.50(1) continued to exclude Irish citizens from the definition of "alien" and voting rights of Irish citizens resident in the UK remained unchanged.

20.2. Commonwealth Citizens

All qualifying Commonwealth citizens are eligible to register for Parliamentary and local elections in the UK. 'Qualifying Commonwealth citizen' means any Commonwealth citizen with leave to remain in the UK or any Commonwealth citizen who does not require leave to remain.[301]

The *Representation of the People Act 1918* was the first act to define the right to vote primarily in terms of simple residence in a constituency. Historically aliens had been excluded from voting by common law and section 9(3) of the RPA 1918 confirmed this by providing that registration could be afforded only to 'British subjects'. (i.e., any person who owed allegiance to the Crown). In 1918 mass immigration had not occurred, and although most of the old Commonwealth countries were already independent, they did not seek to establish their own citizenship until after the Second World War. Thus the status of British subject remained crucial; the concept originates in common law and was based on allegiance to the Crown rather than an accident of birth in a particular place. The *British Nationality and Status of Aliens Act 1914* put into general statutory form that "any person born within His Majesty's dominions and allegiance...shall be deemed to be natural-born British subjects."

In *The Electoral system in Britain* Robert Blackburn comments that the *British Nationality and Status of Aliens Act 1914* was refined by the *British*

Nationality Act 1948 'to replace the notion of common nationality with a system of reciprocal citizenship. It also provided a system whereby countries such as India and the African republics were still to be regarded, for nationality purposes and the right to vote, as 'British subjects', even though they no longer owed allegiance to the Crown but retained their position within the Commonwealth with the British monarch being recognised as Head of the Commonwealth.'[302]

The *British Nationality Act 1981* restricted the term 'British subject' to two extremely limited categories. Accordingly the *Representation of the People Act 1983* refers to the franchise as encompassing Commonwealth citizenship, using the term in the broad sense envisaged by the *British Nationality Act 1948*. The Government gave assurances during the passage of the *British Nationality Act 1981* that the new definition of British subject would not alter the possession of civic rights and privileges such as the right to vote. There have been no plans subsequently to restrict the voting rights of Commonwealth citizens legally resident in the UK who have not acquired British citizenship.

In 1982 the Home Affairs Select Committee reviewed the voting rights of Commonwealth and Irish citizens as part of an investigation into the *Representation of the People Acts* and recommended no change:

> 30. Though the historical background is different, the evidence put forward on behalf of Commonwealth and Irish citizens has many common elements. Both groups are arguing for the maintenance of their existing civic rights, rather than seeking new ones; and both feel threatened by the expression of opinions in certain quarters that these rights should be diminished or removed. In neither case did such a proposal find a voice in evidence to ourselves, and it would seem therefore that there is no widespread public demand for the removal of the voting rights of either Commonwealth or Irish citizens.
>
> 31. We recommend that the civic rights arising out of the status established by the British Nationality Act 1948 and the Ireland Act 1949 should not be disturbed. We do not accept the argument that those seeking to retain the right to vote should be obliged to apply for registration or naturalisation as British citizens. There are a number of practical and emotional considerations which lead us to believe that such a requirement would be unduly harsh, and we appreciate the particular difficulties facing Indian citizens who are not allowed to maintain dual nationality. We are also very conscious of the damaging repercussions which any decision to restrict existing voting rights would have for our relationships both with Commonwealth countries and with Ireland.

32. For all these reasons, we support the Home Secretary in resisting calls for the disfranchisement of any group of citizens within the UK who at present enjoy the right to vote.[303]

21. TIMELINE

1254	First county representatives summoned to English Parliament.
1265	First borough representatives summoned to English Parliament (borough franchises varied).
1429	English county franchise restricted to 40 shilling freeholders.
1542	Welsh counties and boroughs included in English Parliament with franchises matching those of England.
1707	Scottish counties and boroughs included in Parliament of Great Britain. County franchise limited and borough MPs chosen by burgh councils not local electorate.
1800	Irish counties and boroughs included in Parliament of the UK. Separate franchises in counties and boroughs, similar to England.
1832	Reform Acts for England and Wales, Scotland, and Ireland altered the qualifications for voting but retained the different qualifications between county and borough franchise.
1850	Parliamentary franchise in Ireland extended and registration reformed.
1867	Second Reform Act for England and Wales extended the Parliamentary franchise to most householders in Parliamentary boroughs. The county franchise was extended by lowering the property threshold.
1868	Second Reform Act for Scotland and Ireland. Scotland had similar changes to England and Wales but also includes 2 new university seats. In Ireland limited extension of the borough franchise.
1872	Voting by secret ballot begins.
1884	Third Reform Act extended the household franchise to the counties. First Reform Act to apply to the whole of the UK

1918	*Representation of the People Act 1918* gave most women over the age of 30 the vote and created universal male suffrage. Absent voting for some voters allowed and general elections held on a single day.
1928	*Representation of the People (Equal Franchise) Act 1928* equal universal adult suffrage for those 21 years and over.
1948	*Representation of the People Act 1948* abolished plural voting and university seats.
1969	*Representation of the People Act 1969* extends the vote to 18 year olds.
1983	*Representation of the People Act 1983* consolidated existing electoral law and continues to form the basis of current electoral law
1985	*Representation of the People Act 1985* allowed overseas voters to register for Parliamentary elections for the first time (for 5 years after leaving the UK) and allowed any UK voter to apply for postal/proxy votes if unable to vote in person
1989	*Representation of the People Act 1989* increased the time period overseas voters could remain registered to vote in Parliamentary elections to 20 years
2001	*Representation of the People Act 2000* allowed postal/proxy votes on demand. Voters no longer had to give a reason (arrangements introduced in February 2001)
2002	*Political Parties, Elections and Referendums Act 2000* reduced the qualifying period for overseas voters to be registered to 15 years (the change took effect on 1 April 2002)

REFERENCES

Bindoff, ST. *The House of Commons 1509-1558,* History of Parliament Trust, 1982.

Blackburn, Robert. *The Electoral System in Britain,* 1995.

Cook, Chris and Stevenson, John. *British Political Facts 1760-1830,* 1980.

Cowman, Krista. *Women in British Politics,* 2010,.

Dymond, Glenn. *The Life Peerages Act 1958,* House of Lords Library Note LLN 2005/011.

Fisher, DR. *The House of Commons, 1820-1832,* History of Parliament Trust, 2009.

Gash, Norman. *Politics in the Age of Peel: A study in the Technique of Parliamentary Representation 1830-1850,* 2 Ed, 1977.

Gleadle, Kathryn and Richardson, Sarah (Editors). *Women in British Politics, 1760-1860: The Power of the Petticoat,* 2002.

Grant, Raymond. *The Parliamentary History of Glamorgan 1542-1976,* 1978.

Hollis, Patricia. *Ladies Elect: Women in English Local Government 1865-1914,* 1987.

Hostettler, John and Block, Brian. *Voting in Britain, A History of the Parliamentary Franchise, 2001*

Jones, Clive (ed). *A Short history of Parliament,* 2009.

Morris, Homer Lawrence. *Parliamentary Franchise Reform in England from 1885 to 1918,* 1921.

O'Leary, Cornelius. *The Elimination of Corrupt Practices in British Elections 1868-1911,* 1962.

Philbin, J. Holladay. *Parliamentary Representation 1832, England and Wales,* 1965.

Porritt, Edward. *The Unreformed House of Commons: Parliamentary Representation Before 1832,* 1963.

Pugh, Martin. *Electoral Reform in War and Peace 1906-18,* 1978.

Purvis, Matthew. *Members of the House of Lords: Voting at Parliamentary Elections,* House of Lords Library Note LLN 2012/022.

Seager, J Renwick. *Registration of Voters Under the Reform Act 1918,* 1918 Charles Seymour, *Electoral Reform in England and Wales,* 1915.

Smith, FB. *The Making of the Second Reform Bill,* 1992.

Takayanagi, Mari. *Parliament and Women c1900-1945,* A thesis submitted in fulfilment of the requirements of King's College London for the degree of Doctor of Philosophy, 2012.

Thorne, RG. *The House of Commons 1790-1820,* History of Parliament Trust, 1986.

White, Isobel. *Armed Forces Voting,* House of Commons Library Standard Note SN04276.

White, Isobel. *Overseas Voting,* House of Commons Library Standard Note SN05923.

White, Isobel. *Prisoners' Voting Rights,* House of Commons Library Standard Note SN01764.

White, Isobel and Parker, Andrew. *Speaker's Conferences,* House of Commons Library Standard Note SN04426.

Wilding, Norman and Laundy, Philip. *An Encyclopaedia of Parliament,* 4th Ed, 1971.

Williams, WR .*Parliamentary History of the Principality of Wales,* 1895.

End Notes

[1] Robert Blackburn, The Electoral System in Britain, 1995, p66

[2] DR Fisher, The House of Commons, 1820-1832, History of Parliament Trust, 2009, Vol I, p233

[3] FWS Craig, British Parliamentary Election Results 1832-1885, 1977, p624

[4] FWS Craig, British Parliamentary Election Results 1885-1918, 1974, p584 and p588

[5] Chris Cook and John Stevenson, British Political Facts 1760-1830, 1980, Chapter 5, pp115-6

[6] FB Smith The Making of the Second Reform Bill, 1992, pp236-7

[7] Robert Blackburn, The Electoral System in Britain, 1995, p75

[8] Ibid

[9] The Living Heritage pages on the UK Parliament website give more detail of the evolution of Parliament from its Anglo-Saxon origins.

[10] Clive Jones (ed), A Short history of Parliament, 2009, pp7-11

[11] Frederic A Youngs Jnr, Guide to the Local Administrative Units of England, Vol I Southern England, 1980, pxii

[12] JS Roskell, The House of Commons 1386-1421, Vol I, 1993, History of Parliament Trust, p40

[13] Ibid,

[14] Edward Porritt, The Unreformed House of Commons: Parliamentary Representation Before 1832, 1963 Vol I, p547

[15] House of Commons, Returns of Parliament, Ordered to be printed 1 March 1878

[16] Edward Porritt, The Unreformed House of Commons: Parliamentary Representation Before 1832, 1963 Vol I, p502

[17] John Hostettler and Brian Block, Voting in Britain, A History of the Parliamentary Franchise, 2001, pp27-9

[18] Ibid, pp29-30

[19] Kathryn Gleadle and Sarah Richardson (Editors) Women in British Politics, 1760-1860: The Power of the Petticoat, 2002, chapter 1 by Elaine Chalus, p20

[20] Ibid, pp19-38

[21] A burgage was a tenure whereby lands or tenements in cities and towns were held of the king or other lord, for a certain yearly rent (Source: OED). The rent did not have to be in cash and the tenures were varied. In some pre-1832 Parliamentary boroughs the burgage gave the male householder the right to vote at Parliamentary elections. In Old Sarum it was the burgage tenure of a ploughed field gave the right to vote.

[22] Edward Porritt, The Unreformed House of Commons: Parliamentary Representation Before 1832, 1963 Vol I, p40

[23] Kathryn Gleadle and Sarah Richardson (Editors) Women in British Politics, 1760-1860: The Power of the Petticoat, 2002, see chapter 1 by Elaine Chalus, pp19-38

[24] Zoe Dyndor, Widows, Wives and Witnesses: Women and their involvement in the 1768 Northampton Borough Parliamentary Election, Parliamentary History, Vol 30, pt 3, pp309-23

[25] Ibid, pp314-5

[26] Ibid, p319

[27] Ibid, p323

[28] These were defined as "county or other territory in England...as having a ruler with royal privileges and judicial authority (within the territory) which elsewhere belong to the sovereign alone" (Source: http://www.oed.com/ accessed 18 September 2012)

[29] J Holladay Philbin, Parliamentary Representation 1832, England and Wales, 1965, pp17 & 67

[30] Edward Porritt, The Unreformed House of Commons: Parliamentary Representation Before 1832, 1963 Vol I, p20

[31] John Hostettler and Brian Block, Voting in Britain, A History of the Parliamentary Franchise, 2001, p9

[32] JS Roskell, The Commons in the Parliament of 1422, 1954, p5

[33] John Hostettler and Brian Block, Voting in Britain, A History of the Parliamentary Franchise, 2001, p11.

[34] Ibid, p12

[35] Edward Porritt, The Unreformed House of Commons: Parliamentary Representation Before 1832, 1963 Vol I, p21 and p24

[36] Charles Seymour, Electoral Reform in England and Wales, 1915, pp123-4

[37] Edward Porritt, The Unreformed House of Commons: Parliamentary Representation Before 1832, 1963 Vol I, p22

[38] Source: Chris Cook and John Stevenson, British Political Facts 1760-1830, 1980, Chapter 5

[39] Charles Seymour, Electoral Reform in England and Wales, 1915, pp48-9

[40] Source: www.oed.com accessed 18 September 2012

[41] Source: www.oed.com accessed 18 September 2012

[42] To avoid payment was to get away 'scot free' – Brewers Dictionary of Phrases and Fables, 1999, p1051

[43] Edward Porritt, The Unreformed House of Commons: Parliamentary Representation Before 1832, 1963 Vol I, p30

[44] J Holladay Philbin, Parliamentary Representation 1832, England and Wales, 1965, p128

[45] Ibid, pp37-8

[46] John Hostettler and Brian Block, Voting in Britain, A History of the Parliamentary Franchise, 2001, p16

[47] Edward Porritt, The Unreformed House of Commons: Parliamentary Representation Before 1832, 1963 Vol I, p35

[48] J Holladay Philbin, Parliamentary Representation 1832, England and Wales, 1965, p216

[49] DR Fisher, The House of Commons, 1820-1832, History of Parliament Trust, 2009, Vol III, pp206-7

[50] J Holladay Philbin, Parliamentary Representation 1832, England and Wales, 1965, p216

[51] DR Fisher, The House of Commons, 1820-1832, History of Parliament Trust, 2009, Vol II, pp208

[52] Ibid, p206

[53] John Hostettler and Brian Block, Voting in Britain, A History of the Parliamentary Franchise, 2001, p20

[54] DR Fisher, The House of Commons, 1820-1832, History of Parliament Trust, 2009, Vol II, p408

[55] Edward Porritt, The Unreformed House of Commons: Parliamentary Representation Before 1832, 1963 Vol I, p41

[56] 23 Henry VI Chapter 14 – An act for Who shall be Knights for the Parliament, the Manner of their Election, the remedy where one is chosen and another returned.

[57] Edward Porritt, The Unreformed House of Commons: Parliamentary Representation Before 1832, 1963 Vol I, pp43-6

[58] Holladay Philbin, Parliamentary Representation 1832, England and Wales, 1965, pp55-6

[59] Chris Cook and John Stevenson, British Political Facts 1760-1830, 1980, Chapter 5, p57

[60] Edward Porritt, The Unreformed House of Commons: Parliamentary Representation Before 1832, 1963 Vol I, Chapter V, pp99-103

[61] W R Williams, Parliamentary History of the Principality of Wales, 1895, piii

[62] ST Bindoff. The House of Commons 1509-1558, History of Parliament Trust, 1982, p264

[63] Raymond Grant, The Parliamentary History of Glamorgan 1542-1976, 1978, p89

[64] 27 Henry VIII chapter 26 – An Act for laws and justice to be ministered in Wales in like form as it is in this Realm

[65] Edward Porritt, The Unreformed House of Commons: Parliamentary Representation Before 1832, 1963 Vol I, Chapter VI, pp104-18

[66] 35 Henry VIII chapter 11 – An Act for the due Payment of the Fees and Wages of Knights and Burgesses for the Parliament, in Wales.

[67] Ibid

[68] Ibid, p118

[69] Edward Porritt, The Unreformed House of Commons: Parliamentary Representation Before 1832, 1963 Vol II, pp25-6

[70] Clyve Jones (editor) A Short History of Parliament, 2009, chapter 21 'The Parliament of Scotland to 1707' by Julian Goodare, pp302-4

[71] Clyve Jones (editor) A Short History of Parliament, 2009, chapter 14, 'The House of Commons 1707-1800', by Bob Harris, pp170-192

[72] Edward Porritt, The Unreformed House of Commons: Parliamentary Representation Before 1832, 1963 Vol II, pp25-6

[73] Source: Chris Cook and John Stevenson, British Political Facts 1760-1830, 1980, Chapter 5

[74] Norman Gash, Politics in the Age of Peel: A study in the Technique of Parliamentary Representation 1830- 1850, 2 Ed, 1977, p37

[75] Clyve Jones (editor) A Short History of Parliament, 2009, chapter 21 'The Parliament of Scotland to 1707' by Julian Goodare, p304

[76] Edward Porritt, The Unreformed House of Commons: Parliamentary Representation Before 1832, 1963 Vol II, pp116-7

[77] Clyve Jones (editor) A Short History of Parliament, 2009, chapter 21 'The Parliament of Ireland to 1800' by Charles Ivar McGrath, pp321-38

[78] For some of the background into discrimination against Catholics see Library Standard Note SN00683, The Act of Settlement and the Protestant Succession,

[79] Edward Porritt, The Unreformed House of Commons: Parliamentary Representation Before 1832, 1963 Vol II, pp220-2

[80] Ibid, p284

[81] Clyve Jones (editor) A Short History of Parliament, 2009, chapter 21 'The Parliament of Ireland to 1800' by Charles Ivar McGrath, pp333

[82] 'William and Mary, 1691: An Act for the Abrogating the Oath of Supremacy in Ireland and Appointing other Oaths [Chapter II. Rot. Parl. pt. 1. nu. 2.]', Statutes of the Realm: volume 6: 1685-94 (1819), pp. 254-257. URL: http://www.british-history.ac.uk/report.aspx?compid =46356 Date accessed: 16 May 2012

[83] Robert Blackburn, The Electoral System in Britain, 1995, p187

[84] Edward Porritt, The Unreformed House of Commons: Parliamentary Representation Before 1832, 1963 Vol II, pp 290-1

[85] DR Fisher, The House of Commons, 1820-1832, History of Parliament Trust, 2009, Vol I, pp170-1

[86] Ibid, pp170-1

[87] DR Fisher, The House of Commons, 1820-1832, History of Parliament Trust, 2009, Vol I, pp148-51

[88] Ibid, p150

[89] Ibid, pp467-71

[90] Edward Porritt, The Unreformed House of Commons: Parliamentary Representation Before 1832, 1963 Vol II, p334

[91] DR Fisher, The House of Commons, 1820-1832, History of Parliament Trust, 2009, Vol I, pp469-529

[92] RG Thorne, The House of Commons 1790-1820, History of Parliament Trust, 1986, Vol I, pp102-5

[93] Representation of the People Act 1832, (2 Will 4, chapter 45)

[94] John Hostettler and Brian Block, Voting in Britain, A History of the Parliamentary Franchise, 2001, chapter 10 'Victory', pp193-213

[95] Kathryn Gleadle and Sarah Richardson (Editors) Women in British Politics, 1760-1860: The Power of the Petticoat, 2002, chapter 1 by Elaine Chalus, p20

[96] Norman Gash, Politics in the Age of Peel: A study in the Technique of Parliamentary Representation 1830- 1850, 2 Ed, 1977, p86

[97] John Hostettler and Brian Block, Voting in Britain, A History of the Parliamentary Franchise, 2001, chapter 10 'Victory', pp164

[98] DR Fisher, The House of Commons, 1820-1832, History of Parliament Trust, 2009, online version accessed 18 December 2012

[99] Charles Seymour, Electoral Reform in England and Wales, 1915, p23

[100] Norman Gash, Politics in the Age of Peel: A study in the Technique of Parliamentary Representation 1830- 1850, 2 Ed, 1977, p87

[101] Edward Porritt, The Unreformed House of Commons: Parliamentary Representation Before 1832, 1963 Vol I, pp25-8

[102] Charles Seymour, Electoral Reform in England and Wales, 1915, pp107-8

[103] Norman Gash, Politics in the Age of Peel: A study in the Technique of Parliamentary Representation 1830- 1850, 2 Ed, 1977, p88

[104] Charles Seymour, Electoral Reform in England and Wales, 1915, p5

[105] An Act to amend the Law for the Registration of Persons entitled to Vote etc., (6&7 Victoria chapter 18)

[106] Ibid, pp118-22

[107] Report from the Select Committee on Registration of County Voters; together with the proceedings of the committee, minutes of evidence, appendix, and index, HC 203 1864, paragraph 2

[108] Charles Seymour, Electoral Reform in England and Wales, 1915, pp366-7

[109] Parliamentary and Municipal Registration Act 18178 (41 & 42 Victoria chapter 26)

[110] Richard HA Cheffins, Parliamentary Constituencies and their registers since 1832, 17-8, http://www.bl.uk/reshelp/findhelprestype/offpubs/electreg/parliamentary/parliamentaryconstituencies.pdf accessed 17 May 2012

[111] Charles Seymour, Electoral Reform in England and Wales, 1915, p378

[112] Ibid, pp381-3

[113] Local Elections in Britain by Colin Rallings and Michael Thrasher. Routledge, 1997, p22

[114] Robert Blackburn, The Electoral System in Britain, 1995, pp74-5

[115] See History of Parliament Trust publication by DR Fisher, The House of Commons, 1820-1832, History of Parliament Trust, 2009, Vol I, Chapter IX for detailed explanations of some of the variations. The pages are available on line http://www.historyofparliamentonline.org/volume/1820-1832/survey/ix-english-reformlegislation

[116] DR Fisher, The House of Commons, 1820-1832, History of Parliament Trust, 2009, Vol I, Chapter IX, p389

[117] Ibid, p395

[118] Ibid, p393

[119] Ibid, pp389-91

[120] Ibid, p69

[121] Ibid, p404

[122] Ibid, pp404-5

[123] Norman Wilding and Philip Laundy, An Encyclopaedia of Parliament, 4th Ed, 1971, p564

[124] John Hostettler and Brian Block, Voting in Britain, A History of the Parliamentary Franchise, 2001, p215

[125] Norman Gash, Politics in the Age of Peel: A study in the Technique of Parliamentary Representation 1830- 1850, 2 Ed, 1977, pp12-3

[126] John Hostettler and Brian Block, Voting in Britain, A History of the Parliamentary Franchise, 2001, pp210-1

[127] Ibid, p211

[128] Cornelius O'Leary, The Elimination of Corrupt Practices in British Elections 1868-1911, 1962, p15

[129] A person is guilty of treating if either before, during or after an election they directly or indirectly give or provide any food, drink, entertainment or provision to corruptly influence any voter to vote or refrain from voting. Treating requires a corrupt intent – it does not apply to ordinary hospitality (Source: Electoral Commission Summary of electoral offences)

[130] Ibid, pp15-6

[131] Ibid, p16

[132] Charles Seymour, Electoral Reform in England and Wales, 1915, pp115-6

[133] An Act to Amend the Representation of the People in Scotland (2 & 3 William IV chapter 65)

[134] Norman Gash, Politics in the Age of Peel: A study in the Technique of Parliamentary Representation 1830- 1850, 2 Ed, 1977, p36

[135] Norman Gash, Politics in the Age of Peel: A study in the Technique of Parliamentary Representation 1830- 1850, 2 Ed, 1977, p48

[136] DR Fisher, The House of Commons, 1820-1832, History of Parliament Trust, 2009, Vol I, p146

[137] An Act to Amend the Representation of the People of Ireland (2 & 3 William IV chapter 88)

[138] Norman Gash, Politics in the Age of Peel: A study in the Technique of Parliamentary Representation 1830- 1850, 2 Ed, 1977, pp53-4

[139] DR Fisher, The House of Commons, 1820-1832, History of Parliament Trust, 2009, Vol I, p213

[140] Ibid, p215

[141] Ibid, p215

[142] HC Deb 1 May 1848, Vol 98 c584-9

[143] Ibid, c586

[144] Ibid, c587-8

[145] Ibid, c589

[146] Representation of the People 1867, (30 & 31 Victoria. chapter 102)

[147] Charles Seymour, Electoral Reform in England and Wales, 1915, p174

[148] Ibid, p235

[149] Ibid, p241

[150] Ibid, pp241-7

[151] Ibid, pp250-6

[152] Representation of the People Bill 1867, Bill 79

[153] FB Smith, The Making of the Second Reform Bill, 1992, gives a full account of the passage of the both Gladstone and Disraeli's Bills.

[154] University Elections Act 1861 (24 & 25 Victoria chapter 53)

[155] FB Smith The Making of the Second Reform Bill, 1992, pp236-7

[156] Ibid, p236

[157] Charles Seymour, Electoral Reform in England and Wales, 1915, p286

[158] FB Smith The Making of the Second Reform Bill, 1992, p236

[159] FB Smith The Making of the Second Reform Bill, 1992, pp225-6

[160] Ibid, pp226-7

[161] Ibid, p228

[162] FWS Craig, British Parliamentary Election Results 1832-1885, 1977, pp540 and 547

[163] Ibid, p552

[164] FB Smith The Making of the Second Reform Bill, 1992, p236

[165] Sections 5 and 6, Representation of the People in Scotland Act (31 & 32 Victoria chapter 48)

[166] FB Smith The Making of the Second Reform Bill, 1992, p236

[167] Section 8 Representation of the People in Scotland Act (31 & 32 Victoria chapter 48)

[168] Representation of the people (Ireland) Bill, Bill 71 of 1868

[169] FB Smith The Making of the Second Reform Bill, 1992, p236

[170] FB Smith The Making of the Second Reform Bill, 1992, p228

[171] Section 8, Representation of the People in Ireland Act 1868 (31 &32 Victoria chapter 49)

[172] FB Smith The Making of the Second Reform Bill, 1992, p228

[173] John Hostettler and Brian Block, Voting in Britain, A History of the Parliamentary Franchise, 2001, p145

[174] HC Deb 27 May 1862 vol 167 c60

[175] HC Deb 2 July 1862, vol 167 c1310

[176] Charles Seymour, Electoral Reform in England and Wales, 1915, p429

[177] House of Commons, Report from the Select Committee on Parliamentary and Municipal Elections, March 1870, HC 115, pp4-5

[178] Ibid, p3

[179] Ibid, p8

[180] Ibid,

[181] Charles Seymour, Electoral Reform in England and Wales, 1915, p432

[182] The Parliamentary and Municipal Elections Act 1872 Part 1(2)

[183] JA Cannon, Oxford Companion to British History, 2009, "Corrupt Practices Act", Online version accessed 22 May 2012

[184] Ibid, p419-426

[185] Cornelius O'Leary, The Elimination of Corrupt Practices in British Elections, 1868-1911, 1962, pp132-3,159-61

[186] Charles Seymour, Electoral Reform in England and Wales, 1915, p385

[187] Law Commission. Electoral Law in the United Kingdom, A scoping consultation paper, 15 June 2012, pp7-8

[188] Representation of the People Act 1884 (48 Victoria, chapter 3)

[189] Boundary Commission for England and Wales Report, C 4287, 1885

[190] Redistribution of Seats Act 1885 (48 & 49 Vict chapter 23)

[191] HC Deb 28 February 1884, vol 285 c120

[192] HC Deb 28 February 1884, vol 285c110

[193] Representation of the People Act 1884 (48 Victoria, chapter 3)

[194] Robert Blackburn, The Electoral System in Britain, 1995, p74-5

[195] House of Commons, Electors (counties and boroughs). Return showing, with respect to each division of a county and each county in England and Wales etc. 1886 (44-Sess.2)

[196] Homer Lawrence Morris, Parliamentary Franchise Reform in England from 1885 to 1918, 1921, p10

[197] HC Deb 26 May 1884, c1395-1407

[198] HC Deb 27 March 1884, c932

[199] House of Commons Information Office, archived Factsheet M4, Women in the House of Commons.

[200] Key dates and an overview of women and the vote is available on the UK Parliament's Living Heritage pages.

[201] UK Parliament, Women and the vote Key Dates. Constance Rover, Women's Suffrage and Party Politics in Britain 1866-1914 Appendices I and II details the coverage and progress women's suffrage Bills in the period

[202] Homer Lawrence Morris, Parliamentary Franchise Reform in England from 1885 to 1918, 1921, p28

[203] Ibid

[204] HC Deb 20 May 1867, c817-29

[205] An Act for Shortening the Language used in Acts of Parliament (13 & 14 Victoria chapter 21)

[206] Homer Lawrence Morris, Parliamentary Franchise Reform in England from 1885 to 1918, 1921, pp28-9 cites the court case, 1868 Chorlton v Lings, 4 CP 374

[207] UK Parliament, Early suffragist campaigning

[208] See Patricia Hollis, Ladies Elect: Women in English Local Government 1865-1914, Chapter 1 which describes the local franchise for women and how campaigners for women's suffrage encouraged women's participation in local government

[209] Patricia Hollis, Ladies Elect: Women in English Local Government 1865-1914, 1987, p31

[210] Ibid, p39

[211] Ibid, pp31-3

[212] Krista Cowman, Women in British politics, c1689-1979, 2010, pp51-5

[213] HC Deb 10 June 1884, c1943

[214] HC Deb 12 June 1884, c206

[215] Homer Lawrence Morris, Parliamentary Franchise Reform in England from 1885 to 1918, 1921, p86

[216] Ibid, p95

[217] Ibid, p107

[218] Krista Cowman, Women in British Politics, 2010, pp73-4

[219] Ibid, pp75-6

[220] Ibid, p76

[221] Homer Lawrence Morris, Parliamentary Franchise Reform in England from 1885 to 1918, 1921, p85

[222] Ibid, p86

[223] Ibid, p107

[224] Ibid, p118

[225] Martin Pugh, Electoral Reform in War and Peace 1906-18, 1978, p50

[226] Ibid, pp120-1

[227] Ibid, p123

[228] HC Deb 19 July 1916, c1074-5

[229] Homer Lawrence Morris, Parliamentary Franchise Reform in England from 1885 to 1918, 1921, pp124-5

[230] HC Deb 16 August 1916, c1891

[231] HC Deb 14 December 1916, c988

[232] HC Deb 16 August 1916, c1949

[233] For more background on Speaker's Conferences see Library SN/PC/04426 Speaker's Conferences. See also Chapter IX of Homer Lawrence Morris's, Parliamentary Franchise Reform in England from 1885 to 1918, 1921, which gives a thorough commentary on the establishment of the Conference through to the passing of the Bill.

[234] Martin Pugh, Electoral Reform in War and Peace 1906-18, 1978, pp71-2

[235] Homer Lawrence Morris, Parliamentary Franchise Reform in England from 1885 to 1918, 1921, pp129-30

[236] Martin Pugh, Electoral Reform in War and Peace 1906-18, 1978, pp71-2

[237] Conference on Electoral Reform, Letter from Mr Speaker to the Prime Minister, 27 January 1917, Cd 8463

[238] Representation of the People Bill 1917-18, Bill 49

[239] Homer Lawrence Morris, Parliamentary Franchise Reform in England from 1885 to 1918, 1921, p134

[240] Homer Lawrence Morris, Parliamentary Franchise Reform in England from 1885 to 1918, 1921, p157

[241] John Hostettler and Brian Block, Voting in Britain, A History of the Parliamentary Franchise, 2001, p355

[242] J Renwick Seager Registration of Voters Under the Reform Act 1918, 1918, p3

[243] Homer Lawrence Morris, Parliamentary Franchise Reform in England from 1885 to 1918, 1921, p137

[244] JIbid, p156

[245] Ibid, p6 and p12

[246] Schedule 9 Part III, Representation of the People Act 1918

[247] Homer Lawrence Morris, Parliamentary Franchise Reform in England from 1885 to 1918, 1921, pp104-2

[248] HC Deb 19 June 1917, c1751-2

[249] Homer Lawrence Morris, Parliamentary Franchise Reform in England from 1885 to 1918, 1921, pp146

[250] John Hostettler and Brian Block, Voting in Britain, A History of the Parliamentary Franchise, 2001, p355

[251] Ibid

[252] House of Commons Library Standard Note SN04276 Armed Forces Voting gives more detail on the subsequent developments with armed forces voting

[253] John Hostettler and Brian Block, Voting in Britain, A History of the Parliamentary Franchise, 2001, p151

[254] Ibid, p151

[255] HC Deb c29 March 1928, c1471

[256] Ibid

[257] Mari Takayanagi, Parliament and Women c1900-1945 chapter 4. This paragraph is reproduced with kind permission

[258] Ibid, c1367

[259] HC Deb 29 March 1928, c1359-1481

[260] House of Commons Library, SN/PC/04426 Speaker's Conferences, p5

[261] House of Commons Library, SN/PC/04426 Speaker's Conferences, p6

[262] HC Deb 18 November 1968, c913-4

[263] HC Deb 18 November 1968, c915-6

[264] HC Deb 26 November 1968, c424

[265] Further reduction of the age at which people can vote is discussed in Library Standard Note SN01747 Voting Age

[266] House of Lords Library, Library Note 2012/022 Members of the House of Lords: Voting at parliamentary Elections, June 2012, p1

[267] Ibid, p2

[268] Ibid, pp2-3

[269] Ibid, p3

[270] Ibid, p3

[271] House of Lords Library Note LLN 2005/011, The Life Peerages Act 1958, p2

[272] Explanatory Notes: Electoral Administration Act 2006

[273] Section 73 Electoral Administration Act 2006

[274] HL Deb 6 February 2006, c1028-9

[275] HL Deb 15 May 2006, c122-4

[276] Electoral Commission, Managing electoral registration in Great Britain: guidance for Electoral Registration Officers , paragraph 5.3, part B, page 12

[277] House of Commons Library, Standard Note SN01764, Prisoners' Voting Rights

[278] John Hostettler and Brian Block, Voting in Britain, A History of the Parliamentary Franchise, 2001, p20

[279] J Renwick Seager, Registration of Voters Under the Reform Act 1918, 1918, p35

[280] Ibid

[281] More detail is given in Library Standard Note SN01674 Prisoners' Voting Rights

[282] Robert Blackburn, The Electoral System in Britain, 1995, p81

[283] HL Deb 2 December 1982, c1313

[284] HC Deb 2 February 1983, c391

[285] HC Deb 8 February, c896 and HL Deb 8 February, c1150

[286] Law Commission, Electoral Law in the United Kingdom: A scoping consultation paper, p1

[287] Ibid

[288] http://lawcommission.justice.gov.uk/areas/electoral-law.htm accessed 28 August 2012

[289] Law Commission, Electoral Law in the United Kingdom: A scoping consultation paper, p1

[290] See House of Commons Library Standard Note SN05923 Overseas Voters for more detail

[291] HC 32 1982-3, para 27

[292] Cmnd 9140 January 1984

[293] For more detail on the extension of the Parliamentary franchise to British citizens living overseas see Library Standard Note SN05923 Overseas voters

[294] Electoral Commission News release, Expat Brits risk losing their say at general election, 22 September 2009

[295] Library Standard Note SN05923 Overseas voters, p9

[296] Library Standard Note SN03667 Postal voting and electoral fraud gives a brief history of postal voting

[297] There are similar regulations for Scotland and Northern Ireland. However the postal voting changes did not take place in Northern Ireland due to continuing concerns about electoral abuse. For more information about elections in Northern Ireland see Library Research Paper 05/15, The Electoral Registration (Northern Ireland) Bill [HL], available at http://www.parliament.uk/briefing-papers/RP05-15

[298] Library Standard Note SN03667 Postal voting and electoral fraud, p4

[299] Memorandum submitted by the Home Office in Representation of the People Acts. First Report of the Home Affairs Committee, Session 1982-83 (HC 32-II, 1982-83).

[300] HC Deb 11 May 1949, c1855.

[301] Electoral Commission website, Voter Registration, accessed 24 July 2012

[302] Robert Blackburn, The Electoral System in Britain, by Robert Blackburn,1995

[303] HC 32, 1982/83

In: A History of Voting Rights ...
Editor: Nicole P. Springer

ISBN: 978-1-62948-870-7
© 2014 Nova Science Publishers, Inc.

Chapter 2

OVERSEAS VOTERS[*]

Isobel White and Richard Cracknell

INTRODUCTION

British citizens living overseas are entitled to be registered to vote in UK Parliamentary elections for up to 15 years in the constituency they were registered in before leaving the UK. They are not entitled to vote in UK local elections or elections to the devolved assemblies.

There have been calls for the 15 year rule to be changed, most recently during the passage of the *Electoral Registration and Administration Act 2013* but the Government has indicated that it has no plans to alter the arrangements for overseas voters at the moment.

Harry Shindler, a British citizen who has lived in Italy since 1982, and who has therefore not been able to vote in UK Parliamentary elections since 1997, took his case to the European Court of Human Rights in 2009 and argued that no time limit should be imposed on the right of British citizens living overseas to vote in the UK. In its judgment on 7 May 2013, the European Court ruled that there had been no violation of Article 3 of Protocol No 1 (right to free elections) of the European Convention on Human Rights and determined that the UK had legitimately confined the parliamentary

---

[*] This paper (House of Commons Library Standard Note SN05923) was published by the House of Commons Library (United Kingdom) October 14, 2013. The paper contains Parliamentary information licensed under the Open Parliament Licence v1.0.

franchise to those citizens who had 'a close connection to the UK and who would therefore be most directly affected by its laws.'

This Note provides background to the provisions relating to overseas voters in the *Representation of the People Act 1985* which was subsequently amended by the *Representation of the People Act 1989* and the *Political Parties, Elections and Referendums Act 2000*. Information is also given about the procedure for registering to vote as an overseas elector and the means of voting, either by post or by proxy.

There are different arrangements for the armed forces and these are covered in Library Standard Note SN/PC/4276, *Armed forces voting*.

1. BACKGROUND

Before 1985 British citizens resident outside the United Kingdom were unable to register to vote in UK Parliamentary elections. The *Representation of the People Act 1985* extended the franchise to British citizens resident outside the UK and enabled them to register as 'overseas voters' in the constituency for which they were last registered. This was initially for a period of 5 years, this was later extended to 20 years by the *Representation of the People Act 1989*, and then reduced to 15 years by the *Political Parties, Elections and Referendums Act 2000*.

1.1. The Representation of the People Act 1985

During the 1970s there was pressure to extend the franchise to British citizens living and working abroad. Representations were made to the Speaker's Conference on Electoral Law in 1973-4, but the Conference did not make any specific recommendations. The Home Affairs Select Committee subsequently recommended in 1983 that all UK citizens resident in EEC countries should have the right to vote in British Parliamentary elections.[1] The Government response to the Committee's report recommended a seven year limit, noting that 'in the Government's view a person's links with the United Kingdom are likely to have weakened significantly if he has lived outside it for as long as ten years'.[2] The Government also recommended that the right be extended to British citizens living in non EEC countries, saying that it would find it hard to defend provisions giving British citizens the right to vote in Paris, but not in New York.

There was a period of consultation before legislative proposals were brought forward; the *Representation of the People Act 1985* subsequently made provision for British citizens resident overseas to remain on the electoral register in the UK for a period of 5 years.

1.2. The Representation of the People Act 1989

The level of overseas registration under the 1985 Act was far lower than expected despite overseas publicity. Some of the apparent lack of enthusiasm for the new scheme was attributable to its practical complications, including the need for the elector to take all the steps to register without reminders. The Conservative manifesto for the 1987 election promised to extend the period of eligibility, but was not specific about a new time limit.[3]

A period of consultation of all interested bodies followed, with a consultation paper issued in April 1988.[4] This suggested a new time limit of between 7 and 20 years, or even an unlimited qualification. In the Parliamentary session 1988-89, a further Bill was introduced to extend and simplify the scheme. Some of the qualifying aspects, such as requiring attestation by a consular official, were removed. The Bill, as introduced, proposed a 25 year period, but this was reduced to 20 years following amendments which were accepted by the Government. The *Representation of the People Act 1989* therefore made provision for a 20 year limit for overseas voters.

1.3. Home Affairs Select Committee Report October 1998

The Home Affairs Select Committee published a report, *Electoral Law and Administration*, in October 1998. The Committee considered the provisions of the *Representation of the People Act 1985* relating to overseas voters and took the view that the twenty year period within which a British citizen living overseas could retain the right to vote was excessive and recommended that the earlier limit of five years should be restored. In evidence to the Committee, the Labour Party and the Liberal Democrats both argued that twenty years was perhaps too long a period but the Home Office reported that most of the correspondence it had received on the issue was not from people calling for the twenty year period to be lowered but from people resident abroad for more than twenty years arguing for it to be increased.

1.4. The Political Parties, Elections and Referendums Act 2000

There was initially a provision in the *Political Parties, Elections and Referendums Bill 1999- 2000* to reduce the limit to 10 years. During the passage of the Bill amendments were proposed to review this new limit and in the House of Lords at committee stage, the Government suggested increasing the proposed limit from 10 years to 15 years. This meant a reduction of five years on the *status quo*. An amendment to create a 15 year limit was subsequently passed unopposed.[5] This provision, in s141 of the *Political Parties, Elections and Referendums Act 2000*, took effect from 1 April 2002 and is still in place.

The Labour Government did not subsequently indicate any plans to extend the 15 year limit but there were calls to increase the registration rate amongst British citizens living abroad.

The Electoral Commission launched campaigns to encourage British citizens abroad to register to vote in UK elections. In 2009 the Commission issued a press release describing its campaign before the forthcoming general election:

> There are more than 5 million British citizens living abroad, but only a few thousand of them have registered to vote in the upcoming UK general election...
>
> British citizens living abroad can register as overseas voters if they have been registered to vote in the UK at any time within the past 15 years. Yet of the estimated 5.5 million British citizens living abroad, less than 13,000 overseas voters are currently on a UK electoral register.
>
> Brits living overseas can vote by post or arrange for a proxy to vote for them in a UK Parliamentary election and the Commission has launched a campaign to encourage British citizens abroad to register to vote ahead of the next general election.

Jenny Watson, Chair of the Electoral Commission, said:

> "British citizens living abroad come from a wide variety of backgrounds, but we know that most maintain strong links with the UK. It is easier than ever before for British citizens abroad to keep in touch with friends, family and colleagues back home and many will also want to have their say in elections.[6]

2. REGISTRATION OF OVERSEAS VOTERS

Overseas voters cannot register to vote if they have never been registered as a voter in the UK but if a voter left the UK before they were 18 they can be registered at their parents' or guardians' address provided that they left the UK no more than 15 years ago.

Overseas voters have to register to vote each year in the same way as voters living in the UK. The first time an overseas voter makes an application to be included on the register their declaration that they are living overseas must also be accompanied by an attestation by a British citizen. The Electoral Registration Officer will send the overseas voter a renewal form each year until the end of the 15 year period. Overseas voters can vote by post or proxy, or in person at their allotted polling station if they are in the UK at the time of the election.

The Electoral Commission recommends that overseas voters should consider appointing a proxy to vote on their behalf because of the short period available to be sent and return a postal vote overseas.

If the overseas voter is serving in the armed forces, or is a Crown servant, there are different provisions for registering to vote as they are not subject to the 15 year rule. Briefly, members of HM forces and their spouses can either register by means of a service declaration or can choose to be registered as an ordinary elector instead. A service declaration is valid for five years and then has to be renewed.[7]

Crown servants and British Council employees employed in a post outside the UK, together with their spouses, are also entitled to be registered for all elections and have to submit a Crown Servant or British Council declaration with their application to register.

The Electoral Commission's website gives further details about the registration of overseas voters and a link to the relevant registration forms.[8]

3. LENGTHENING THE ELECTORAL TIMETABLE

There has been concern that there is insufficient time in the Parliamentary election timetable for postal ballot papers to be sent out to and be returned by overseas voters in time for the election.

3.1. General Election 2010

The Commission's report on the administration of the 2010 general election made the following comments on the effect of the short Parliamentary timetable on overseas voting:

> 5.33 British citizens living overseas who had moved to another country within the last 15 years, and who had previously been registered in the UK, could register to vote in the UK general election as an 'overseas voter'. Overseas voters could choose to vote by post or appoint a proxy.
>
> 5.34 Some overseas voters who had registered for a postal vote have complained that they did not receive their postal ballot packs in time to vote in the election, or that they did not receive them at all. The election timetable meant that postal ballot packs could only be issued after 20 April 2010 at the earliest, leaving two weeks for ballot packs to be received by electors based overseas, completed and returned to Returning Officers in the UK before 10pm on 6 May.
>
> 5.35 It was clear at this election that the tight timescale for the issue and return of overseas postal votes meant that some people were not able to return their postal ballot packs in time for their votes to be counted. The UK Government must take into account these concerns as it considers rationalising the election timetable as part of its planned introduction of fixed-term elections for the UK Parliament.[9]

3.2. House of Lords Debate on 2 March 2011

A short debate in the House of Lords on voting arrangements for British citizens living overseas and members of the armed forces serving abroad was held on 2 March 2011. Viscount Astor asked whether the government would consider changing the voting arrangements that were currently in place; he suggested that it was very difficult for British citizens living abroad to register and even more difficult for them to successfully use their postal votes. Lord Astor noted that 'the only sure way for members of the armed forces to vote is by proxy' and he continued:

> We seem to be the only EU country that does not encourage its citizens living abroad to play an active part in their own country. It is difficult to register and it is difficult to vote. You have to register in the constituency where you last lived in the UK, and you have to prove it, so many do not bother-it is a cumbersome procedure.[10]

Lord Astor also called on the government to look again at the 15 year rule. Lord Lester of Herne Hill agreed and made the point that a number of British citizens who worked abroad in international organisations did not have the same voting rights as members of the armed forces, Crown servants and employees of the British Council who were not subject to the 15 year cut off rule.[11] Lord Lester had previously asked the government to legislate to change the rules (see the Parliamentary Question below).

Lord Roberts of Llandudno criticised the general election timetable as being too short to allow for postal votes to be sent abroad and returned in time to be counted. This issue was also raised by Baroness Gale who suggested that electronic voting would overcome these problems.[12]

Lord Lexden commented on the number of Conservative Party associations abroad and said that when these associations are asked why so few British citizens living abroad were registered to vote the response was usually that 'the process of registration is too complex and cumbersome.'[13] Baroness Gale also commented on the low registration numbers for British citizens living overseas despite campaigns by the Electoral Commission, most recently in the spring of 2010, to encourage registration.[14]

The Minister, Lord McNally, acknowledged that the Government should address the issue of overseas voters; he said that of an estimated 5.5 million British citizens living abroad, only about 30,000 actually vote. The Government was looking at the length of the election timetable 'with a sense of urgency' and that although there was not a great deal of enthusiasm for it at present, there was a case for a study of electronic voting in the UK. Lord McNally said the issues raised in the debate were substantial and there should be a 'really radical look at voting for our overseas residents and, very importantly, for our military' early in this Parliament.[15]

3.3. 2011 Referendum on the Voting System

Overseas voters were able to vote in the referendum on the voting system on 5 May 2011 because the franchise for the referendum was the UK Parliamentary franchise and peers. The Electoral Commission issued a press release on 2 March 2011 to remind British citizens living overseas that the deadline to register to vote was 14 April 2011. The Commission instructed Counting Officers to send out ballot papers to overseas voters as soon as possible after that date but noted in its report on the referendum that it was concerned that

...the current timetable does not allow sufficient time for overseas electors to apply for, receive and return their postal vote in time for it to be counted. There is little incentive for overseas electors to participate if they cannot be confident that their vote will arrive in time to be counted.[16]

3.4. The Electoral Registration and Administration Act 2013

The Electoral Commission had long recommended that the Parliamentary election timetable should be lengthened to bring it into line with the local election timetable.

The Commission's reasoning was based on the increasing practice of combining local and general elections but also on the benefits for absent voters that a longer timetable would bring. The *Electoral Registration and Administration Act 2013* has subsequently made provision for the Parliamentary election timetable to be extended from 17 to 25 days. The Government has indicated that the provision will be brought into force at the time of the scheduled polls in 2014.[17]

4. NUMBER OF OVERSEAS VOTERS

The table and chart below show the number of overseas electors on the register for each year since 1987; this was the first year for which data was recorded, following the *Representation of the People Act 1985* which first allowed British citizens resident abroad to register.

The number of overseas electors peaks in the years when there is a general election (with the exception of 1991) before falling again over the next few years. The very large increase in numbers of overseas electors in 1991 can be attributed to measures in the *Representation of the People Act 1989* which extended the period during which overseas voters could be registered to vote in UK Parliamentary elections from 5 years to 20 years. There was also a particularly large increase in the number of overseas electors in 2010, and a decline in the following year.

Table 1. Overseas electors on UK electoral register, 1987-2012

Date	Overseas Electors on Register
Feb-87	11,100
Feb-88	2,092
Feb-89	1,836
Feb-90	1,237
Feb-91	34,454
Feb-92	31,942
Feb-93	22,131
Feb-94	18,552
Feb-95	17,934
Feb-96	17,886
Feb-97	23,583
Feb-98	17,315
Feb-99	13,677
Feb-00	10,669
Feb-01	11,496
Dec-01	13,009
Dec-02	9,185
Dec-03 [i]	8,374
Dec-04	9,672
Dec-05	18,947
Dec-06 [ii]	15,090
Dec-07	14,330
Dec-08	13,695
Dec-09	14,901
Dec-10	32,739
Dec-11	23,388
Dec-12	19,120

Sources: ONS, Electoral Statistics and personal communication General Register Office for Scotland, Electoral Statistics Electoral Office for Northern Ireland, personal communication OPCS, Electoral Statistics;   HC Deb 18 Mar 2010 c1031W; HC Deb 10 Sep 2008 c1965W; HC Deb 7 Apr 2005 c1573W; HC Deb 8 Jul 2003 c733W; HC Deb 28 Oct 1999 c962W

Notes:

[i] 2003 figure includes 24 overseas electors registered in Northern Ireland at February 2004; data for Northern Ireland for December 2003 are not available.

[ii] 2006 figure is approximate.

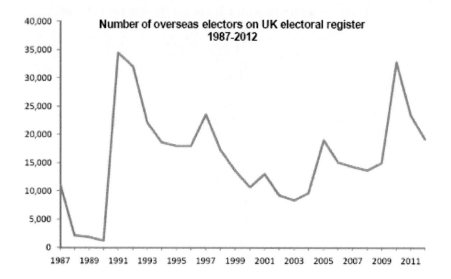

5. REPRESENTING OVERSEAS CONSTITUENTS

There is no specific guidance for MPs on constituency correspondence with expatriates, nor are there any legal restrictions on how a Member of Parliament undertakes their duties. In his evidence to the Modernisation Committee's 2007 inquiry into the role of the back bench Member, the Clerk of the House wrote that "How backbenchers perform their role as Members of the House is largely a matter for each Member to decide".[18]

How Members carry out their duties is a matter for them to determine individually. The *Code of Conduct for Members of Parliament* simply states that Members have a "special duty" to their constituents.[19]

The convention that Members should only handle casework on behalf of their own constituents does not go beyond that bald outline. It offers no advice to individual Members as to how they should undertake such casework, as the following extract from the Standard Note on *Members and Constituency Etiquette*[20] demonstrates:

> "The simple, general principle is that any citizen in the United Kingdom should first get in touch with his own constituency representative".[21] Edmund Marshall, formerly MP for Goole, so wrote in the fullest account, yet to appear, about the practicalities of a Member's dealings with his constituents. He continued:

There is a convention, almost universally observed on all sides of the House of Commons, that Members deal with personal inquiries only from their own constituents.[22]

The corollary of this is that when a Member is contacted by someone who is not her or his own constituent, that person should be referred without delay to the constituency Member.[23]

There have been suggestions that there should be a MP specifically for British citizens living overseas; similar suggestions for a MP for the armed forces serving abroad have also been made. It is doubtful whether such proposals would be supported by the present Government which has already legislated to reduce the number of Members in the House of Commons.[24] It is also sometimes difficult for MPs for British citizens living abroad to assist with problems raised by their constituents which concern the government and administration of the country in which they live and where the UK Government has no jurisdiction; having MPs for specific areas overseas would not solve this dilemma.

6. POSSIBLE FUTURE CHANGES TO THE 15 YEAR RULE

There have been calls for the Government to reconsider the 15 year rule. The issue was raised recently during the passage of the *Electoral Registration and Administration Bill 2012- 13* in the House of Commons. Geoffrey Clifton-Brown (Conservative) proposed that a new clause should be added to the Bill to remove the 15 year rule. Mr Clifton-Brown explained the reasons for his amendment to the Bill:

> According to the Institute for Public Policy Research, 5.6 million British citizens currently live abroad. The shocking truth is that although, as of last December, about 4.4 million of them were of voting age, only 23,388 were registered for an overseas vote, according to the Office for National Statistics' electoral statistics. Out of 4.4 million potential overseas voters, only 23,000-odd are actually registered! Half the problem is the difficulties of the registration process, which I brought before the House during the clause 1 stand part debate on 18 June, but the other half of the problem is the cut-off limit or qualifying period.[25]

The Parliamentary Secretary, David Heath, replied that the Government would give the issue 'serious consideration' but that it would not rush into a decision 'not because of any wish to obstruct, but simply because the question of extending the franchise is a fundamental one, and both the Government and the House would have to feel comfortable with doing that'.[26] The amendment was subsequently withdrawn.

The Bill received its second reading in the Lords on 24 July 2012 and Lord Norton of Louth raised the issue of overseas voters during the debate:

> ...although there are 4.4 million British citizens of voting age living abroad, only just over 23,000 are registered as overseas voters... I appreciate the reasons for not wishing to rush to judgement. There are practical issues as well as the issue of principle raised by the Minister-the two come together in terms of ensuring the integrity of the ballot. However, there is a countervailing principle in respect of the rights of those who, while they may live abroad, retain British citizenship. It will be helpful if my noble friend gives some indication of the Government's thinking in the light of the discussions in the other place.[27]

Lord Lexden also called for the 15 year rule to be abolished:

> There are some, such as Mr Clegg, who are inclined to say that our fellow country men and women abroad should take the nationality of the country in which they reside, even though I understand that Mrs Clegg, who retains Spanish nationality, has a lifetime's right to vote in Spain's elections. There are others who say that because they pay no taxes here they should not vote here, but many do pay taxes. In any case, other countries do not admit taxation as a principle for access to their franchises. Others say that our fellow citizens abroad cannot feel a strong attachment to the United Kingdom after some years away from it. However, in the age of the internet, they can follow closely what is happening in their native land and, as online participants, contribute powerfully to developments taking place here whether they live in Perugia, Portugal or Pennsylvania.
>
> I set out the case for change more fully in a debate initiated by the noble Lord, Lord Wills, in January and I propose to return to it in Committee. The Government have this great issue under active consideration, as the Minister confirmed in a Written Answer to me on 25 June. There could be no better time for action than in this Diamond Jubilee year. Some 5.6 million subjects of Her Majesty live abroad. Many of them today stand hopefully at the bar of British democracy. Let all those who wish to join us be allowed to enter.[28]

Lord Wallace of Saltaire responded for the Government and said there were no plans to extend the 15 year rule:

I had a conversation off the Floor of the House with the noble Baroness, Lady Hayter, in which we agreed that we are both being lobbied heavily by our local party organisations from Brussels and Luxembourg on this issue. The Government does not have any plans at the present moment to lengthen the period from leaving the country beyond 15 years, nor do we have any really ambitious plans to do what is done in some other countries, which is to allow voting in embassies and consulates. However, the longer electoral period will help.[29]

The issue was raised again during consideration of the Bill at Report stage in the House of Lords when Lord Lexden moved another amendment to insert a new clause which would extend the fifteen year time period. The amendment was withdrawn after Lord Wallace responded that the Government had listened to the arguments but had decided that:

There are large questions here about what rights we might grant, for how long and for how many people we might grant them, and whether we should grant them for people who were born abroad. We might appropriately consider these questions, but, I suggest, not in the context of the Bill.[30]

Lord Wallace also suggested that an all-party inquiry into the issue might be the best way forward.

A Parliamentary Question answered in February 2013 confirmed that the Government has no immediate plans to make changes to the legislation:

Iain Stewart: To ask the Deputy Prime Minister what plans he has to review the rights of overseas electors to vote in general elections.

Miss Chloe Smith: British citizens resident overseas can register to vote in UK parliamentary and European parliamentary (but not local) elections in the UK, provided that they have been registered in the UK in the past 15 years.

The Government is considering whether the 15-year limit into voting rights for British citizens overseas remains appropriate, but has no immediate plans to alter the legislation.[31]

7. ALL-PARTY WORKING GROUP
ON OVERSEAS VOTING

In June 2013 an all party working group on overseas voting was launched with Lord Norton as its Chair. Various blogs for overseas voters have referred to the Group.[32]

8. RULING OF THE EUROPEAN COURT
OF HUMAN RIGHTS 7 MAY 2013

Harry Shindler, a British citizen who has lived in Italy since 1982, has long fought for a change in the law to allow him to vote in UK Parliamentary elections.

He first took his case to the European Court of Human Rights in 2009 and has argued that no time limit should be imposed on the right of British citizens living overseas to vote in the UK.[33]

In its judgment on 7 May 2013, the European Court of Human Rights ruled that there had been no violation of Article 3 of Protocol No 1 (right to free elections) of the European Convention on Human Rights and decided that the UK's electoral law 'had not gone too far in restricting the right to Mr Shindler's right to free elections'.[34]

The Court also found that:

> ...allowing non-residents to vote for 15 years after leaving the country was not an unsubstantial period of time. Having regard to the significant burden which would be imposed if the United Kingdom were required to ascertain in every application to vote by a non-resident whether the individual had a sufficiently close connection to the country, the Court was satisfied that the general measure in this case promoted legal certainty and avoided problems of arbitrariness and inconsistency inherent in weighing interests on a case-bycase basis.
>
> The Court concluded, having regard to the margin of appreciation available to the United Kingdom in regulating its parliamentary elections, that the restriction imposed on Mr Shindler's right to vote was proportionate to the legitimate aim pursued.[35]

End Notes

[1] HC 32 1982-3, para 27.

[2] Cmnd 9140 January 1984.

[3] The Next Steps Forward 1987.

[4] Dep NS 3902 see HC Deb 29 April 1988 c 285-6W.

[5] HL Deb 22 November 2000 c924.

[6] Electoral Commission press release, 22 September 2009.

[7] For further details see Library Standard Note SN/PC/4276.

[8] http://www.aboutmyvote.co.uk/register_to_vote/british_citizens_living_abroad.aspx.

[9] Report on the administration of the 2010 UK general election, Electoral Commission, July 2010.

[10] HL Deb 2 March 2011 c1119.

[11] HL Deb 2 March 2011 c1123.

[12] HL Deb 2 March 2011 c1131.

[13] HL Deb 2 March 2011 c1126.

[14] HL Deb 2 March 2011 c1130.

[15] HL Deb 2 March 2011 c1133.

[16] Referendum on the voting system for UK Parliamentary elections: report on the May 2011 referendum, Electoral Commission, October 2011, p71.

[17] HC Deb 12 July 2013 c421W.

[18] Modernisation Committee, Revitalising the Chamber: the role of the back bench Member, 20 June 2007, HC 337 2006-07, Evidence from the Clerk of the House of Commons, Ev 97.

[19] House of Commons, Code of Conduct, June 2009, HC 735 2008-09.

[20] House of Commons Library Standard Note SN/PC/2028, Members and Constituency Etiquette, 30 January 2012.

[21] Edmund Marshall, Parliament and the Public, 1982, p21.

[22] Ibid, pp21-22.

[23] The House of Commons provides a constituency locator in order to deduce in which constituency a particular address falls, http://findyourmp.parliament.uk/

[24] Parliamentary Voting System and Constituencies Act 2011.

[25] HC Deb 27 June 2012 c346.

[26] HC Deb 27 June 2012 c353 and 354.

[27] HL Deb 24 July 2012 c642.

[28] HL Deb 24 July 2012 c659.

[29] HL Deb 24 July 2012 c680.

[30] HL Deb 23 January 2013 c1130.

[31] HC Deb 12 February 2013 c693W.

[32] http://votes-for-expat-brits-blog.com/2013/06/27/send-your-evidence-to-all-party-inquiry-on-overseas-voting/ http://www.votes-for-expat-brits.com/

[33] WWII veteran loses ruling on expats voting in UK elections, BBC News, 7 May 2013.

[34] Right to vote of British national who has lived outside the UK for thirty years not violated by UK election laws, European Court of Human Rights press release, 7 May 2013.

[35] ibid.

In: A History of Voting Rights ...   ISBN: 978-1-62948-870-7
Editor: Nicole P. Springer   © 2014 Nova Science Publishers, Inc.

Chapter 3

ARMED FORCES VOTING*

Isobel White

1. THE REPRESENTATION OF THE PEOPLE ACT 1918

"War, so often the midwife of reform, led to the most comprehensive Representation of the People Act that had yet been seen."[1]

The changes incorporated in the Representation of the People Bill 1917-18 included universal suffrage for men on the basis of residence; up to that point it had been linked directly or indirectly to the payment of rates. The vote was given to graduates of provincial universities, and women over thirty were enfranchised if they were local government electors or the wives of local government electors. Owners and tenants were included in the local franchise, but the vote was not extended to all residents. David Butler explains the provisions enabling servicemen to vote after World War I in his book *The Electoral System in Britain Since 1918*:

> Votes were given to servicemen on easier terms, as far as residence was concerned. Those who had served in the war were entitled to vote at the age of nineteen. Conscientious Objectors, on the other hand, were disenfranchised for five years.[2]

---

* This is an edited, reformatted and augmented version of the House of Commons Library Standard Note SN04276. The paper contains Parliamentary information licensed under the Open Parliament Licence v1.0, dated July 12, 2011.

For the first time there were arrangements made to deal with the problem of the absent voter; service men and others unable to vote in person at a poll were put on the absent voters list:

> For the immediate post war period servicemen overseas were to be entitled to vote by post, and permanent arrangements were made for proxy voting by servicemen.[3]

Butler describes the end of the special arrangements for counting the service vote:

> In 1920 after some agitation, the Government decided to abandon the postal voting provisions laid down in the Act of 1918. The special provisions delaying the count for eight days to allow for the return of ballots from servicemen overseas had been necessary enough at the end of the war, but, in subsequent by-elections, there had been a steadily diminishing number of postal votes, and annoyance at the delay in announcing the result had grown.[4]

The *Representation of the People (No2) Act 1920* provided that postal voting should be limited to the United Kingdom; servicemen abroad could appoint proxies who would be able to vote for them on their behalf.

2. THE REPRESENTATION OF THE PEOPLE ACT 1948

The *Representation of the People Act 1945* had again made temporary provision for postal voting by service voters. Strenuous efforts were made by the Government to get all servicemen to complete their claim forms to be included on the service register, and it was announced that 90 percent had done so.[5] This appears to have been an exaggeration, as there were apparently 4,682,000 men in the forces on 30th June 1945[6] and hardly more than 1 million can have been under twenty one, but only 2,895,000 were on the service register. Of those on the service register, only 1,701,000 succeeded in recording their votes (59 per cent). Only half of those who had appointed proxies had votes recorded on their behalf and a quarter of those who applied for postal ballots were found not to be on the service register.[7]

The timetable of the 1945 general election was altered because of the need to allow time for the service register to be compiled and for the service ballots to be returned. The election was announced on 27 May, but polling day was not until 5 July and counting of the votes did not take place until 26 July. Butler commented that 'it was thus the most protracted election since the institution of a single nationwide polling day.'

Preparations for a comprehensive Representation of the People Act were made in December 1946. The arrangements for electoral registration in peace conditions were considered by a Home Office committee that had been set up a year earlier. Since members of the forces would have to make a claim submitting the name of their proxy, it was thought that there was little point in providing automatic registration but that everything should be done to help servicemen and seamen to get onto the register.

No recommendation was made about postal voting for servicemen overseas but if there was to be time for ballots to be sent out and returned, the consequent delays in conducting the election were highlighted by the committee. It concluded that servicemen in the United Kingdom should be allowed to vote by post or proxy as before.

The subsequent *Representation of the People Act 1948* granted postal voting facilities to both service personnel and to certain groups of civilians, including those who were physically incapacitated, those unable to vote without making a journey by sea or air or because of the nature of their occupation, and those who were no longer residing at their qualifying address. All had to provide an address in the UK to which ballot papers could be sent. Service personnel could, alternatively, vote by proxy if they were likely to be at sea or abroad on polling day.

3. THE REPRESENTATION OF THE PEOPLE ACT 2000

Before 2001 all members of HM Forces had to register as service voters. This registration remained effective until the elector made a new declaration or left the Forces. The *Representation of the People Act 2000* ended this arrangement:

> **7.** Section 12(3) and (4) of the 1983 Act (by virtue of which persons with service qualifications may only be registered in pursuance of a service declaration, even where they would otherwise be entitled to be registered by virtue of residence in the United Kingdom) shall cease to have effect.[8]

The provision gave effect to the recommendation of the Working Party on Electoral Procedures which recommended that members of the armed forces, and their families, should be able to register at their home address rather than solely by means of a service declaration.[9]

The Service Indices were closed in February 2002 which meant that there was no longer a central body holding the details of all registered service voters. *The Representation of the People Act 2000* allowed for postal voting on demand and Service voters serving abroad could now choose whether to vote by post or by proxy. Previously they had to vote by proxy if they were overseas as there was no provision for postal votes to be sent abroad.

MPs raised concerns in PQs about the level of armed forces registration following the changes in the law. On 10 January 2005, during Defence Questions, Ivor Caplin, the Parliamentary Under-Secretary of State for Defence, told James Gray MP:

> We are working closely with the Electoral Commission to improve awareness in the service community of the options to register to vote. An internal information campaign will begin in the next few weeks to coincide with the publication of a new Defence Council instruction providing full information and practical help on how to register and explaining the various voting options.[10]

Ivor Caplin had also responded to a short adjournment debate in Westminster Hall on 8 December 2004 which had been initiated by Andrew Tyrie MP. Both he and Peter Viggers MP had reported a decline in the number of armed forces personnel registering to vote in their constituencies.[11]

In the debate the Minister outlined the changes that had been made to the way in which service personnel registered to vote and the rationale for those changes:

> The changes were considered likely to encourage more service personnel to use their votes and to register with an up-to-date address, whether by means of a service declaration or in the standard way, instead of the one at which they had lived when they first joined the services. The changes also meant that the names of service declarants did not remain indefinitely on other electoral lists long after the people concerned had left the armed forces.
>
> All service personnel and their partners have the option to register as service voters by completing a yearly service declaration form, which should be returned to the relevant local council electoral registration office. When registering in that way, a service voter's qualifying address

is the address in the United Kingdom at which they would be living if they were not in the services. The advantage of that option is that their registration remains constant even if they are moved from one location to another on a tour of duty.

Since 2000, service personnel and partners have had other options on how to register as electors in line with civilian electors. If they live at a permanent address in the United Kingdom, either at a private or qualifying address, or at service families accommodation or single living accommodation, a serviceman or woman can register as a conventional voter.

For those personnel and their partners who are posted abroad and who do not wish to register as service voters, there is the option of registering as overseas electors. That facility is available to all British citizens who live abroad but have been registered as electors in Britain within the past 15 years. The disadvantage of that option to service personnel is that overseas electors can take part only in United Kingdom parliamentary and European parliamentary elections. They do not qualify to vote in local council elections.[12]

Measures were being put in place to inform service personnel of the options they had in registering to vote:

> … All ships, units and stations are instructed to give personnel and their dependants, especially those who are overseas, every reasonable assistance to register as voters. Defence Council instructions direct that all new entrants to the armed forces be made aware of the procedures and options for registering as voters. I can confirm that our personnel are also notified of all parliamentary elections.
>
> The Ministry of Defence issues annually a Defence Council instruction explaining the procedures for registration. That instruction is sent to 2,300 addresses, which include ships and shore establishments, all major units and independent sub-units. The Defence Council instruction is in the final stages of revision, and will be republished early in the new year. It will also be made available to service personnel via the Department's website. Obviously, our discussions with the Electoral Commission may determine some of what is said in the instruction.[13]

A number of press articles before the general election of 2005 reported a low rate of registration amongst the armed forces and that consequently many service personnel would be unable to vote on 5 May 2005:

> Tens of thousands of men and women in the Armed Services are not eligible to vote in the election because they were unaware that they had to

register. The estimated yesterday that up to 80 per cent of military personnel would be unable to vote. They said leaflets on how to register were sent out too late for overseas personnel to register by the March 11 deadline, and the Army website carried out-of-date information which was not corrected until early February. Soldiers, sailors and airmen used to register for elections just once in their career, but since 2001 they have had to register every year.

Although they can register at their home addresses, most join as service voters. The Electoral Commission produced 110,000 leaflets for troops. However, some of those stationed overseas said they did not get them in time.

Andrew Robathan, Conservative defence spokesman, conducted a straw poll while in Iraq in February and found that eight out of 10 troops had not registered and had no idea that they had to. He said the Electoral Commission was "patently not interested in making sure that people serving their country are able to vote". There are more than 200,000 British servicemen and women, around 48,000 of whom are currently stationed or deployed overseas.

The Electoral Commission said that the leaflets had been printed and sent to the Ministry of Defence by the start of February for distribution via the forces postal system. Tabitha Cunniffe, of the Electoral Commission, said: "The delay was at the MoD's end. There is now no opportunity for anyone who has missed the deadline, but it is something we will be looking into for the next election."

The shadow defence secretary, Nicholas Soames, said: "It is scandalous that the same servicemen and women who made it possible for the Iraqi elections to take place are denied their right to vote by the feckless incompetence of Labour ministers."

Lord Garden, a Lib Dem defence spokesman, said: "It's rather sad that we send our military personnel off to establish democracy and set up elections in countries like Iraq and Afghanistan, but don't make enough arrangements for them to vote here."

A MoD spokesman said that all units had received the leaflets by the middle of February, allowing plenty of time to register. She said: "We are not aware of anyone not having received the leaflets in time. There was also information on services broadcasting and the internal website."[14]

3.1. Joint Inquiry of the Constitutional Affairs and ODPM Select Committees into Electoral Registration

The joint inquiry of the Constitutional Affairs and ODPM Housing, Planning, Local Government and the Regions Select Committees into electoral registration acknowledged the growing concern about the fall in the numbers of armed forces personnel registering to vote.[15] The Committees' report, published in March 2005, stressed that it was essential that the Ministry of Defence should play an active role in encouraging service personnel to register and made the following recommendation:

> We expect the MOD to monitor the effectiveness of its revised Defence Council Instruction issued in late January 2005 on electoral registration and report the results to Parliament. It is already too late for service personnel to register for the local elections or any general election on 5 May 2005, but we recommend that the MOD adopt a policy of issuing annual individual registration forms to each service person to encourage them to register. We expect the MOD to look into the issue of electoral registration among service personnel as a matter of urgency and we urge the relevant select committees in the next parliament to follow it up.[16]

3.2. 'Silence in the Ranks': Paper Published by the Army Rumour Service Website

In September 2005 a paper was published by the 'Army Rumour Service' website about the problem of under-registration amongst the armed forces. *Silence in the ranks: an analysis of factors inhibiting electoral participation by HM Forces personnel and their families in the General Election of May 2005, with recommendations on the way forward* was submitted to the Electoral Commission, the Ministry of Defence and the then Department for Constitutional Affairs.[17] The Army Rumour Service drew attention to the lack of accurate information available to the armed forces about how they could register to vote in time to participate in the general election and had revealed that 'the Electoral Commission leaflets which were intended to be circulated in early February 2005 did not actually reach any service personnel until the week beginning 4 March 2005. Many personnel did not see it – if at all – until after the registration deadline on 11 March.'[18] The Army Rumour Service also found that some local authority websites contained out of date information or no specific information for service voters and that the Ministry of Defence website did not have adequate information about registration and voting options for members of the services and their spouses.

The Army Rumour Service monitored problems experienced by armed forces voters at the general election; some voters were not able to vote because of the late arrival of ballot papers which made returning them in time impossible. Three main factors were identified in the late arrival of postal ballot papers:

> (1) The UK's tight electoral timetable, which meant that no postal ballots could be despatched until 15 days before polling day;
> (2) Late despatch of postal ballots in some council areas, including those for voters overseas or elsewhere in the UK; and
> (3) Postal delays, especially in the BFPO mail system.[19]

The report made a number of recommendations about improving the system of postal voting and supported the then Department for Constitutional Affairs' proposal to make the deadline for postal vote applications 11 days before polling day rather than six, but also suggested that a controlled trial of electronic voting for service voters should be considered.[20] The report also suggested that there should be a survey of electoral registration, experiences and perceptions amongst service personnel and that an information leaflet for service voters should be distributed to every member of the armed forces at the time of the next annual canvass in the autumn of 2005.[21]

On 23 September 2005 the Electoral Commission published a leaflet, *Register to vote: voting information for members of Her Majesty's Armed Forces and their families.* The Times had reported on 21 September that the leaflets were to be sent out to service personnel and that all units would have to appoint an officer responsible for service voting:

> Months after claims that tens of thousands of members of the Armed Forces were disenfranchised at the general election, the Government has promised measures to help them to register to vote. The Ministry of Defence and the Electoral Commission were accused of acting too late after disclosing that they were sending out 400,000 leaflets so that all Service personnel are aware of their rights. In addition all units are to be required to appoint an officer responsible for Service voting for the Armed Forces and their families. Service personnel are told in the leaflet that they must renew their registration every year and that they will be reminded by their registration office when they need to do it. The move was welcomed last night by Andrew Tyrie, Conservative MP for Chichester, who has been leading a campaign to increase voting in the Service community. But he said last night that the handling of the registration of Service voters had been a disgrace. "These people have been putting their lives on the line to try to bring democracy to Iraq. And while they were doing that the Government made virtually no effort to ensure that they could vote at the last election."[22]

4. THE *ELECTORAL ADMINISTRATION ACT 2006*

The *Electoral Administration Bill 2005-06* was introduced in the Commons by the Rt Hon Harriet Harman, Minister of State for Constitutional Affairs on 11 October 2005. There were no provisions relating to service voters included in the Bill.

During the second reading debate in the House of Commons Andrew Tyrie MP (Con) asked:

> What estimate have the Government made of the number of service voters who were unable to vote because they did not make it on to the register at the last election? Could the right hon. and learned Lady also explain why, despite the fact that vigorous representations were made a full nine months before the general election, we still went into the election with those who are trying to bring democracy to Iraq unable even to vote in their own country?[23]

A number was not given by the Government but the Minister, Harriet Harman, said that the Department for Constitutional Affairs, the Electoral Commission, the MOD and the Armed Services were holding meetings to find a solution to the problems faced by service voters.

It was not until 13 February 2006, during the second reading of the Bill in the Lords, that clauses were introduced which made provisions for service voters. The Liberal Democrat Defence Spokesman, Lord Garden, said:

> It is important to remember that when absent voting—both postal and proxy— was first introduced in 1918, it was primarily for servicemen serving overseas. Similar arrangements were made at the end of World War 2. Postal voting was not extended to civilians until 1948. Until 2001, all service personnel had to register as service voters. Once a person had registered, that registration remained effective until he or she changed to a different address or left the Armed Forces. Their dependants could also use the scheme if they so wished.
>
> Following the 2000 Act, service personnel and their families have had to register annually. The central register that looked after who was on the electoral register from the services was then closed. As a result, no one knows how many service people and their dependants fell off voting registers as the years passed and they moved from posting to posting. Electoral registration officers have reported how difficult it is to obtain access at some units despite the Ministry of Defence's view that they should have such access. They are not able to check even whether they are getting registration information at unit level.

I shall not repeat to your Lordships the sorry tale of the lack of urgency by the Ministry of Defence in the run-up to the May 2005 general election. I spoke in detail about that on 26 May 2005 during the debate introduced by the noble Lord, Lord Lipsey, on the workings of the 2005 election. Since then we seem to have had a welcome recognition by the Government that there is a real problem to be solved. [24]

Suggestions of simple reversion to pre 2000 legislation were also addressed by Lord Garden:

Harriet Harman has spoken of "zero tolerance" in the area of voter registration. Yet there does not appear to be a clear consensus on how best to tackle the issue. Some have argued the point made by the noble Baroness, Lady Hanham, in her contribution—that we could return to the pre-2000 position. We could go back to the previous system where service voter registration lasted for someone's service life. It is the "better than nothing" option which some have described as at least a move forward, although in fact it is a move backward. It may be that it is the best we can do, but it would be unfortunate if that were the case. We need to seize the opportunity to make both registration and voting easy for service personnel and their dependants. [25]

Lord Garden went on to raise the issue of communicating changes of legislation to members of the Armed Services and called for the Ministry of Defence to take responsibility for the implementation of a system which would prevent service voters missing their opportunity to vote:

During the May 2005 general election it was not just distant postings in Iraq and Afghanistan that proved impossible, there were reports of problems in Germany and Northern Ireland caused by mail delays over the bank holiday weekend. Nor should we accept the argument that it is the servicemen's fault because they can always opt for a proxy vote. Not only is a proxy vote sometimes difficult to organise, in my view it is not democratic. We have a duty to make it possible for all service people to cast a secret personal vote. That means that the Ministry of Defence will have to provide the necessary logistics. [26]

On the first day of the Lords Grand Committee, Lord Garden moved an amendment to the Bill inserting a new clause which would place the responsibility for ensuring that servicemen registered to vote on the Ministry of Defence. The Parliamentary Under-Secretary of State for the Department of Constitutional Affairs, Baroness Ashton of Upholland, explained why the

Government thought it would be ill advised to simply revert to the pre-2000 position:

> ... I want to talk a little about the pre-2000 Act position, because I know that there are those who feel that a simple solution is to revert to that. I am concerned to clarify some of the problems with the old system, so that, when noble Lords consider what they want to propose, that has been addressed. Members of the Committee will know that when my right honourable friend George Howarth set up a working group—known as the Howarth working group—it recognised that the old system had low registration rates and that there was a problem with service personnel being disassociated from the constituencies in which they were registered. It also concluded that electoral registration officers had problems identifying and communicating with service personnel both during their careers and after they left the service, which led to some of the inaccuracies in the electoral register. That had the potential to increase the likelihood of electoral fraud and, in some areas, could unjustifiably inflate the numbers on the electoral register.[27]

Lord Garden withdrew the amendment but continued to push for the Ministry of Defence to accept responsibility for the implementation of the new legislation:

On 15 May 2006, the Bill began its Lords report stage. The Government had not yet laid any amendments relating to service voting. Baroness Hanham (Conservative) and the Minister, Baroness Ashton of Upholland, debated the reasons for the statistics on voting of service voters. Baroness Hanham said:

> We should notice that the number of service personnel registered has fallen by 120,000 since the 2000 Act. There were 140,000 service voters registered, but at the 2005 election—as far as anyone knew, given the way that registrations are now spattered around the place—only 25,000 members of the Armed Forces were in a position to vote.[28]

Baroness Ashton of Upholland replied:

> Perhaps I may deal with some of the figures cited today. I want to correct the noble Baroness, Lady Hanham, on the figure of 120,000 only because it is important to make the point. While the figure is right, the reason for the fall is that the 2000 Act enabled people to register without making a service declaration. That is why the figure has dropped quite considerably. I hasten to add that I do not seek in any way to diminish the problem, but it is important to know precisely where figures such as this come from.[29]

Baroness Ashton of Upholland promised the House of Lords that the Government would make provisions to improve the situation, and the amendments were withdrawn. At third reading, which took place on 7 June 2006, a Government amendment was brought forward which included a provision to extend the duration of registrations made by a service declaration to up to five years instead of one year. Baroness Hanham continued to press for a requirement for the MoD to implement these changes, and said:

> My amendment does not seek to force people to register or vote. It seeks to force the Ministry of Defence, which has a duty of care towards its very special employees, to ensure that the best opportunity is available to them to vote. The only way that they can guarantee that opportunity is by actively securing the registration of servicemen and women.[30]

Baroness Ashton of Upholland emphasised the individual's responsibility to register to vote:

> The fundamental difference between us is on whom we put the duty or responsibility for this action. The way our electoral law has worked and the way we have always seen the issue of registration is that the duty and responsibility lies with the individual. I recognise entirely what the noble Baroness says about the difference of the employer status of the Armed Forces. Noble Lords will know that there are other employers who perhaps have people overseas, but I recognise and completely accept the particular significance for the Armed Forces. We do not believe it is right to put the onus on the employer, but rather to work with the employer in these particular circumstances to help to enable the individual to accept and respond to his duty and responsibility.
>
> We do not think it is right to treat a government department differently from any other employer as noble Lords could well bring forward other cases involving particular circumstances. We think it is right and proper though that this particular employer should take additional action and be seen to be very positively encouraging people, who carry out for us the most significant of tasks, to register.[31]

Commons consideration of Lords amendments took place on 13 June 2006. The Parliamentary Under-Secretary of State for the Department of Constitutional Affairs, Bridget Prentice, explained the provisions in the Government's amendment:

> Lords amendment No. 6 deals with service registration, which was raised on Second Reading and in subsequent discussions, and we have

responded, I hope, to the points that were made in the House and elsewhere. The amendment includes two key provisions. First, it creates an order-making power to allow the Government to extend the duration of registrations made via a service declaration to up to five years. Current rules require declarations to be reconfirmed annually, so the extension would make the registration process more convenient for service personnel, particularly personnel serving overseas. In addition, the amendment does not require members of the armed forces to register solely through a service declaration. Servicemen and women can still register as ordinary electors if they choose to do so.[32]

The methods by which Service voters would be kept informed of relevant information were also outlined:

> If hon. Members will allow to me complete my explanation of the amendment, they may be reassured that it is a much more progressive and positive way forward. It is part of a package of measures to aid the registration of service personnel that includes closer co-operation between the officer in each unit responsible for electoral registration and the ERO. The MoD will issue every new entrant to the armed forces with an electoral registration form, and it will run campaigns during the annual canvass for service personnel whose service declaration is about to expire. Members of the armed forces will receive reminders in their payslips about the need to register to vote and information such as website addresses and so on. Access to service accommodation will be granted to electoral registration officers. Pilot schemes for on-site polling stations at two separate military establishments took place in this year's local elections in Rushmoor and Westminster. Future campaigns will include a service "Registration Day", which will act as a focal point. Unit registration officers will be pro-actively using all appropriate measures to remind and inform service personnel and their families both of the requirement to register to vote and of the way in which they can do so.[33]

The Shadow Secretary of State for Constitutional Affairs, Oliver Heald, was not satisfied with the wording of the amendment:

> As the Under-Secretary knows, I believe that amendment No. 6 is better than nothing and I congratulate all those, including my noble Friend Baroness Hanham, who managed to wring it out of the Ministry of Defence. However, if she reads further, she will realise that the Ministry of Defence is required to secure "(so far as circumstances permit) an effective opportunity of exercising from time to time as occasion may require the rights" to register and to vote. That is not the same as requiring the Ministry of Defence to effect the registration of servicemen.

I want that to happen. There is a difference between us and I hope that I have made the point clearly. We do not agree and I would therefore like to press amendment (a) to a Division, because our servicemen deserve it.[34]

The Government amendment was agreed to on a division.

5. IMPLEMENTATION OF THE CHANGES MADE BY THE EA ACT 2006

The *Service Voters' Registration Period Order 2006* was debated in the Delegated Legislation Standing Committee on 6 November 2006. The Order changed the period of time that members of the forces (and their spouses or civil partners) who have made a service declaration and are registered or entitled to be registered, from a period of 12 months to a period of 3 years. The order came into force on 1 January 2007.

During the Standing Committee debate Andrew Turner MP (Con) asked the Minister, Bridget Prentice, to explain the reasons for the Government's decision to extend the registration period to 3 years, when the Act would allow an extension of up to 5 years. Bridget Prentice replied:

> We chose 3 years rather than the 5 available under the Act after consultation with the MOD and the Electoral Commission. Three years is the minimum amount of service time for people, so we thought that would be appropriate, but of course the MOD is much more proactive now in ensuring that people continue to be registered.[35]

The Electoral Commission commented on the new arrangements for service voters:

> The Commission welcomes this provision, which extends the duration of a service voter's registration as an elector from 12 months to three years.
> We believe that this measure will serve to address the risk of the under-registration of service personnel by making registration more convenient for service personnel and their spouses – particularly those serving overseas.
> However, we continue to believe that additional measures need to be in place and sustained to ensure that the maximum number of eligible service personnel are registered to vote. We will therefore, continue to

work with the Government, the Armed Forces and the electoral registration officers to devise and implement measures aimed at improving the registration levels of service personnel."[36]

During the passage of the *Political Parties and Elections Act 2009* in the House of Lords an amendment was tabled which, if accepted, would have made the Service declaration indefinite. Lord Bates (Conservative) moved the amendment in Grand Committee and argued that this would address the under-registration of armed services personnel.[37] The Minister, Lord Bach, said that the Ministry of Defence was not in favour of the amendment and that the three year period struck the right balance between encouraging service personnel to register and maintaining an accurate register. However, by report stage the Government had reconsidered the issue and Lord Bach announced that the period of a service declaration would be extended from three years to five.[38]

5.1. The *Service Voters' Registration Period Order 2010*

The Government subsequently consulted the Electoral Commission about the draft *Service Voters' Registration Period Order 2010*. The Commission said that it would support the increase to five years 'if the Ministry of Justice and Ministry of Defence feel that this is appropriate. However, we feel that five years is probably the upper limit for the length of declaration that would be appropriate under the current registration system'.[39]

The *Service Voters' Registration Period Order 2010*, which extends the period for service voters' declarations from 3 to 5 years, was considered and approved by both Houses of Parliament before the general election.[40] In the House of Commons consideration was by the Twelfth Delegated Legislation Committee[41] and in the Lords by the Lords Grand Committee.[42]

The Electoral Commission issued a Circular about the Order.[43] The circular set out the changes to the registration period:

> 4. Until now, members of HM Forces and their spouses or civil partners registering through a service declaration have had to renew their registration every three years. From commencement of The Service Voters' Registration Period Order 2010 on 19 March 2010, the length of registration based on a service declaration is now five years and so, from 19 March 2010, service voters will only need to renew their registration at the end of a five year period.

5. The extension of the length of registration will apply to all service personnel and their spouses or civil partners who register as service voters through a service declaration from 19 March 2010 onwards. It also applies retrospectively to those who are already registered as service voters, which in effect, extends their registration period by a further two years. Electoral Registration Officers will need to amend their records accordingly.

6. Although the service declaration has been extended to five years, given the mobility of service personnel, we continue to recommend that HM Forces service voters are contacted annually to ensure that details such as addresses and absent voting arrangements remain accurate.

5.2. Service Voting Surveys

On 27 June 2007 the Parliamentary Under-Secretary of State for Defence, Derek Twigg, made a written ministerial statement about the results of a survey of service voting by the Defence Analytical Services Agency:

> I have today placed in the Library of the House a copy of the report of a survey on service voting conducted by the Defence Analytical Services Agency in 2006.
>
> The MOD has been working with the Electoral Commission to improve the electoral process for the armed forces. The survey was undertaken to provide evidence of the numbers of Service personnel who are currently registered to vote and to draw comparison with the results of a similar survey carried out in 2005. The surveys provide information which is helping us judge how best to encourage Service personnel to register in future.
>
> I welcome the survey, which gives us the facts needed to target future work. It indicates that 63 per cent. of service personnel are currently registered, in comparison with 60 per cent previously, the majority of whom (65 per cent) choose to register as ordinary rather than Service voters. The number serving abroad who are registered has risen from 36 per cent in 2005 to 42 per cent in 2006.
>
> These figures indicate that registration levels have improved but there is still much work to be done, particularly for those serving abroad; the results will help to indicate where our efforts should be concentrated. We will work closely with the Electoral Commission to understand the reasons behind the results and to use them to make further improvements to the quality of information available to all Service personnel.
>
> We remain committed to improving arrangements for the Service community to exercise their right to vote. We will do this by encouraging our people to register and to vote, and underpin this by clear information

provided in a timely manner. We shall continue to work hard, with the Electoral Commission, to achieve this.[44]

The Defence Analytical *Services Agency's Service Voting Surveys* for 2007 and 2008 were also placed in the Library of the House of Commons.[45] The registration rate in 2007 was 68% and in 2008 it was 65%. However, many service personnel are registered as ordinary voters, rather than service voters. This point was also made in a recent PQ:

> **Mr. Maude:** To ask the Secretary of State for Justice what estimate he has made of the proportion of (a) armed forces personnel and (b) members of the public who are registered to vote.
>
> **Mr. Wills:** No assessment has been made of the proportion of (a) armed forces personnel and (b) members of the public who are registered to vote. This is because the Office for National Statistics (ONS) does not have information on the proportion of the public who are registered to vote, as not everyone who is usually resident is entitled to vote. The total number of full-time armed forces personnel at 1 May 2009 was 194,280.
>
> ONS figures reveal that as of 1 December 2008 the number of armed forces personnel who registered by way of a service declaration was 21,928. Not all armed forces electors, however, register as service voters. They may either register as an ordinary elector, an overseas elector or a service elector. The Ministry of Defence Service Voting Survey 2008 indicates that 75 per cent. of respondents were registered as ordinary voters.
>
> The Government are keen to support armed forces personnel in registering to vote. In order to increase service registration rates, the Government have recently announced that we will increase the service voter declaration period from three years to five years, which we hope will encourage more service personnel to register. We aim to bring forward this change in secondary legislation as soon as possible.[46]

5.3. Service Voter Registration Campaigns in 2007, 2008 and 2009

Since 2007 the Electoral Commission and the Ministry of Defence have carried out service voter registration campaigns in the autumn. Registration leaflets and application forms have been sent out to Service personnel in the UK and across the world and Unit Registration Officers (UROs) have been appointed in all units to provide information about electoral registration. The Electoral Commission and the MoD have also provided additional resources such as posters and PowerPoint presentations to accompany the leaflets. 'Service Electoral Registration Days' have been held at every unit each autumn since 2007. The Electoral Commission asked Electoral Registration Officers to record the number of service registration forms they received back so that it could evaluate the success of the campaigns.

An Electoral Commission press notice gave further details of the 2009 campaign:

> Each year a campaign is run in support of the annual canvass period to provide information to Armed Forces personnel and their families about registration, voting and elections. The current campaign, will run between October and November and is built on the experience of previous campaigns; it will include:
>
> - sending our combined service voter registration leaflet and application form to service personnel in 5,000 military units across the world
> - registration days held in each unit led by a dedicated Unit Registration Officer
> - PR and advertising in service broadcast and print media; and information on our and MoD's websites
> - additional guidance and tools, such as promotional posters and resource CDs delivered to all units
> - encouraging local authority Electoral Registration Officers to work with service representatives to encourage registration[47]

The chair of the Electoral Commission, Jenny Watson, launched the 2009 advertising campaign and warned service personnel not to lose the opportunity to have their voice heard:

> "The next General Election could be called at any time between now and June 2010. If you're serving overseas between now and then, the best way to make sure your vote is counted is to apply for a proxy vote. That means you can ask someone you trust back home, who is also eligible to vote, to vote on your behalf. So why not choose that person now? That way, you're prepared for the election- whatever the date. Or you can register to vote by post. But the tight timescale and logistical challenges involved in getting a ballot paper to you and back home again may make this an unrealistic option. You put your lives on the line for our country. So make sure you have a vote on election day."

MoD research has shown that 35% of service personnel are not registered to vote. Information about registering to vote, including how to apply for a proxy or postal vote, and a downloadable registration form can be found at www.aboutmyvote.co.uk/armedforces[48]

The Electoral Commission also issued a Circular, EC17/2009, to notify Electoral Registration Officers about the service voter registration campaign.[49]

6. VOTING PROCEDURES FOR THE ARMED FORCES

Although registration of armed forces personnel is being addressed there is still a problem with the voting process; there is insufficient time for postal ballots to be sent out to forces serving abroad and for these to be returned by polling day. As Jenny Watson, Chair of the Electoral Commission, noted above, it is usually better for military personnel overseas to appoint a proxy who can vote on their behalf, either at the polling station or by post. The Government reiterated this in an answer to a PQ asked by Lord Roberts of Llandudno on 10 November 2009:

> **Lord Roberts of Llandudno:** To ask Her Majesty's Government whether they propose to ensure that military personnel overseas who are registered for postal voting receive their ballots in sufficient time for them to be returned to be included in constituency counts.
>
> **The Parliamentary Under-Secretary of State, Ministry of Justice (Lord Bach):** Postal votes cannot be issued until the close of nominations, which for a UK parliamentary election means 11 working days before the poll. For this reason the Electoral Commission recommends proxy voting as the best way to ensure service personnel can cast their ballot, and the Commission recently issued guidance to all military personnel to encourage their participation in this way. However, it is important that service personnel have the opportunity to participate in the democratic process, and my right honourable friend Michael Wills MP has written to all MPs inviting them to a meeting to discuss ways in which the registration and voting arrangements for service personnel can be improved.[50]

Lord Roberts asked a similar question in the House of Lords on 9 December 2009 and there was an exchange with the Minister, Lord Bach, during which the Minister announced that the Government was looking at putting a scheme in place whereby the armed forces in Afghanistan could receive and return postal ballot papers in time for them to be counted. This could be done by using the regular supply flights to the forces in Afghanistan.

The Parliamentary Under-Secretary of State, Ministry of Justice (Lord Bach): My Lords, service personnel face unique challenges in electoral participation. The Government are working to ensure that we have in place the most effective measures to support their participation. A registration awareness campaign has engaged every Armed Forces unit, and the Government will extend the service declaration period from three years to five to increase convenience. The Elections Minister met MPs and Armed Forces families' representatives last week to discuss further steps.

Lord Roberts of Llandudno: I am grateful to the Minister for that Answer. I hope that that will include provision that ballot papers will be delivered in plenty to time to servicemen in, say, Afghanistan-9,000 of whom would appreciate the speeding up of thought that the Government are giving to that question. Can I ask two further questions?

Lord Roberts of Llandudno: We are all concerned about this. First, could we have the automatic registration of service recruits, so that they are registered to vote when they sign up to the Armed Forces? Secondly, could we have permanent machinery in place so that we do not always have to fight a battle to make sure that service personnel are able to vote in what are vital elections to them, as they are to the rest of us?

Lord Bach: My Lords, I will do my best in the limited time to answer the noble Lord's first question on this occasion. Statutorily, there are only 11 working days from the close of nominations until polling day. This is a very tight timeframe, which presents logistical challenges for Armed Forces personnel serving overseas. However, for this election we are attempting to put a scheme in place, which will work for troops on active service in Afghanistan. We have been looking at the current postal voting system and we believe that it is possible to set up such a scheme, which would deliver ballot papers to and from Afghanistan in time for them to be counted. Why? Because there are a lot of supply flights to that country on a very regular basis. We are working towards that end. I have to emphasise that operational priorities must prevail at all times and we cannot guarantee success, but I hope the House will think that it is worthwhile trying.

Lord Swinfen: Using modern information technology, would it be possible to have the votes counted confidentially in Afghanistan and the results e-mailed to the relevant constituencies in the United Kingdom, so that they can be incorporated in the final counts?

Lord Bach: The noble Lord puts forward an interesting and ingenious idea, which I will take back. The Elections Minister, my right honourable friend Mr Wills, has set up a working group consisting of officials from the Ministry of Justice, the Ministry of Defence and the Electoral Commission, as well as the families federations of the Armed Forces. It is considering a number of proposals, and I will make sure that that is one of them.[51]

6.1. 2010 General Election

An article in the *Times Online* in March 2010 drew attention to the problems of postal votes for armed forces serving overseas and suggested that the previous government was considering electronic voting for service personnel serving overseas in the future. The article also noted that the 2010 general election (which had not been called when the article was published) would probably coincide with a changeover of troops in Helmand province, thus further complicating the arrangements for postal voting for the troops there.

> The timing of this year's election, widely expected to be on May 6, coincides with the change over of the British brigade in Helmand, a massive logistics exercise which threatens to delay postal services to troops.
> A government source said: "There have historically been problems with postal votes for those in the armed forces deployed overseas.
> "After the current election we intend to have a thorough look at what can be done to ensure all service personnel get their chance to vote.
> "One option we are looking at is e-voting. It would require a change in legislation. It could be rolled out to other groups, but the armed forces would be a priority."[52]

A Parliamentary Question on 6 April 2010, just before dissolution of the 2005 Parliament, sought information about the steps taken to ensure that the armed forces in Afghanistan would be able to cast their votes in the general election:

> To ask Her Majesty's Government what steps they have taken to ensure that all British Armed Forces personnel in Afghanistan will have the opportunity to vote in the forthcoming elections and that their votes will be counted.
> **The Minister for International Defence and Security (Baroness Taylor of Bolton):** My Lords, first, I am sure that the whole House will join me in offering sincere condolences to the families and friends of Guardsman Michael Sweeney of 1st Battalion Coldstream Guards and Rifleman Mark Turner of 3rd Battalion The Rifles, both of whom were killed on operations in Afghanistan recently.
> The Ministry of Defence works closely with the Ministry of Justice and the Electoral Commission to enable those service personnel in Afghanistan who choose to vote by post to do so. We are striving to expedite, subject to operational priorities, the delivery of ballot papers to

and from Afghanistan for service personnel. We have encouraged all
personnel to register to vote and to vote by proxy.
  [...]
  My right honourable friend in another place, Michael Wills,
recognised the potential problem for people voting in Afghanistan. That
is why the Electoral Commission has designed a bespoke registration
form which is being given to people operating in those difficult
circumstances, and special arrangements are being made to dispatch
ballot papers and to return them as quickly as possible. All that, of course,
is subject to operational requirements....
  Lord Roberts of Llandudno: ....I received an official poll card this
morning that says that postal votes will be posted on Friday 23 April and
that, in the case of any difficulty, we are to phone the local registration
office by 30 April. How will forces in Afghanistan and elsewhere be able
to respond to that warning?
  Baroness Taylor of Bolton: My Lords, I recognise the long-term
interest that the noble Lord has taken in this issue, but I had hoped that
registration and encouraging people to vote would not be an issue of
party-political divide at this time. I can think of many other things that
will be, but perhaps not that.
  Special arrangements have been made for those in Afghanistan, as I
said, with a bespoke form. We are in the middle of a roulement - a change
of personnel - in Afghanistan and part of the deployment package
consists of information about registration, the appropriate form and a
recommendation that service personnel in Afghanistan vote by proxy, as
that is the surer way of ensuring that their votes are cast. Those new
arrangements are an improvement and I hope that the whole House will
welcome them.[53]

One of the complicating factors during the 2010 general election
campaign was the closure of UK airspace due to volcanic ash. The Electoral
Commission issued Circular EC 15/2010 which explained that applications for
rolling registration and absent votes would be acceptable by fax or scanned
into an email. There was also an option to change to proxy voting until 5pm on
20 April 2010. The Commission noted:

**Registration of service voters in Afghanistan and requests for
postal votes**

14. We understand from the MoJ that some further registration and proxy
or postal vote applications have been received at Rushmoor Borough
Council from Afghanistan as scanned copies. Andrew Colver is emailing
these to relevant EROs. These copies, as with all other scanned copies of

absent vote application forms that meet the prescribed requirements, should be accepted by EROs.[54]

The Electoral Commission's report on the general election, published in July 2010, referred to the service voter initiative conducted by the MoJ and the MOD:

> 5.31 For the 6 May elections the UK Government put in place new arrangements to support service personnel in Afghanistan to register and to vote. Couriers and dedicated space on military flights were used to speed up the delivery of electoral registration applications and postal ballot packs to and from service personnel based in Afghanistan. The Government was supported by the Head of the Democratic Services Team at Rushmoor Borough Council in England, who acted as a central coordination point for the postal fast-track process.
>
> 5.32 The UK Government has indicated that 294 proxy voting applications were received and forwarded to Electoral Registration Officers through this initiative, and 217 postal votes were successfully returned from Afghanistan to Returning Officers in around 120 local authorities. We expect the Government to carry out a full evaluation of the initiative, and we look forward to considering the results of that evaluation.[55]

6.2. 2011 Referendum on the Voting System

A Parliamentary Question on 18 May 2011 sought information about the numbers of armed forces serving overseas who were registered to vote in the 2010 general election and also in the 2011 referendum on the voting system; how many of them voted by proxy and how many by using a postal ballot. The Minister, Mark Harper, replied:

> No central record is kept of the number of armed forces personnel who registered and voted at either the 2010 UK parliamentary election or the referendum on the voting system earlier this month. Armed services personnel may register to vote as ordinary electors, as service electors or, where appropriate, as overseas electors and therefore it is not possible to readily identify all of them.
>
> However, the Defence Analytical Services and Advice Survey conducted by the Ministry of Defence in 2009 showed that an estimated 69% of service personnel were registered to vote. The report of that survey is available from the Library of the House. The latest survey is

currently being analysed, and a copy will be placed in the Library of the House upon completion by the Minister for Defence Personnel, Welfare and Veterans.

Under targeted initiatives implemented for service personnel who were in Afghanistan during the May 2010 and 2011 polls, service voters were able to register for a proxy or postal vote and specific processes were put in place to support their participation. I understand that for the 2010 UK parliamentary election, 217 postal votes were successfully returned and distributed out to returning officers. In addition to this 294 applications to vote by proxy were received and forwarded to electoral registration officers. The corresponding figures for the referendum on the voting system in 2011 were 40 postal votes and 281 proxies. The use of proxies in such circumstances is recommended by both the Electoral Commission and MoD.

However, it is not possible to know the overall totals of service personnel registered for postal or proxy votes whilst based in Afghanistan as they could have signed up outside the initiative—either as a service voter or as an 'ordinary' elector.[56]

A PQ answered by the on 7 June 2011 described the special arrangements put in place to make provision for service personnel in Afghanistan to register to vote and use proxy or postal votes in 2011:

> The Ministry of Defence (MOD) and the Cabinet Office worked with the Electoral Commission, British Forces Post Office (BFPO) and Royal Mail to make specific provision for service personnel in Afghanistan to register to vote and use proxy or postal votes, 281 service personnel chose to use proxy votes, as recommended by the Electoral Commission and MOD. There were 61 new applications made to vote by post through this initiative and 40 completed ballots were returned through the dedicated system. No special services were provided for British Forces in Germany because service personnel there receive a direct daily service. In Cyprus, special arrangements were put in place to return ballot papers via RAF flights into Brize Norton and then subsequently as a priority despatch into the Royal Mail. For other overseas locations, BFPO identified and fast tracked ballot papers when under their control.[57]

7. HOUSE OF LORDS DEBATE ON 2 MARCH 2011

A short debate in the House of Lords on voting arrangements for British citizens living overseas and members of the armed forces serving abroad was held on 2 March 2011. Viscount Astor asked whether the government would consider changing the voting arrangements that were currently in place; he suggested that it was very difficult for British citizens living abroad to register and even more difficult for them to successfully use their postal votes. Lord Astor noted that the 'the only sure way for members of the armed forces to vote is by proxy':

> This Government have always seen the merits of enfranchisement of British citizens living abroad. However, in recent years, the take-up of overseas registration has been disappointing. I am afraid that one of the reasons was the change of rules enacted by the previous Labour Government. It is now very difficult for British citizens living abroad to register, and it is even more difficult for them successfully to use their postal vote. As a result, registration has plummeted.
>
> Equally, those serving abroad in the Armed Forces have had severe problems getting their postal votes processed. Does my noble friend have any estimate of how many members of the Armed Forces serving overseas successfully managed to vote at the last election? At present, the only sure way for members of the Armed Forces to vote is by proxy. However, surely those who wish to exercise their vote by secret ballot should be able to do so. It is extraordinary that out of all the troops from NATO countries in Afghanistan, who are there to encourage democracy, ours are often denied it[58].

Lord Wills, who was the Minister responsible in the previous government, said that the number of service personnel serving abroad who were registered to vote increased from around 36% in 2005 to 48% in 2008; he also told the House that before the 2010 general election he had secured agreement with the Conservative and Liberal Democrat parties that a consultation would be launched in July 2010 on the options for additional voting channels for service personnel and their families whatever the outcome of the election. He continued:

> This consultation was to have concluded by the end of November last year. The aim was then to reach conclusions on the way forward in the light of that consultation by spring 2011, and to bring forward legislation in 2012 – in time for the next general election.

Lord Roberts of Llandudno was concerned that very few members of armed services serving in Afghanistan voted in the 2010 general election:

> This morning, the MoD confirmed that we have 9,500 troops in Afghanistan. How many of them voted? It says that at the time of the

general election there were 9,000 or 10,000, so this morning I was astonished to receive figures from the Electoral Commission showing that, in the 2010 UK general election, 294 proxy voting applications were received and forwarded to electoral registration officers and 270 postal votes were successfully returned from Afghanistan to returning officers in about 120 authorities. That is out of 9,000 people who are eligible to vote. That is totally disgraceful and is not acceptable in any modern democracy.[59]

Lord Roberts criticised the general election timetable as being too short to allow for postal votes to be sent abroad and returned in time to be counted. This issue was also raised by Baroness Gale who suggested that electronic voting would overcome these problems.[60] Lord Patten stressed that the service vote and its safety

> ...was not some little issue for returning officers, constitution freaks and those interested in the wider shores of constitutional reform. It is absolutely central that the military covenant in future should embody the rights of servicemen to vote in exactly the same way as anyone within the kingdom.[61]

The Minister, Lord McNally, acknowledged that the 'disengagement of the military is not healthy.'[62] The Government was looking at the length of the election timetable 'with a sense of urgency' and that although there was not a great deal of enthusiasm for it at present, there was a case for a study of electronic voting in the UK; he also took

> the point of the noble Lord, Lord Patten, that the military covenant is important and the right to vote on time and in secret should be addressed as part of that covenant. I will certainly take that message back. It is important that we try to encourage our service personnel to vote. The Government are making every effort to encourage participation in the vote on 5 May, not only in Afghanistan but in other British service areas where the British Forces Post Office will make voting in military locations a priority.
>
> As I said, the Government are introducing an initiative for voting on 5 May. The deadline for new postal vote applications and changes to existing votes for the referendum is 5 pm on 14 April. The chief counting officer for the referendum has directed electoral administrators to prioritise postal votes going overseas, to ensure that they are sent out as soon as possible after the deadline for new postal vote applications has passed, with the first issue of postal votes to take place not later than 18

April. That issue will include postal votes for members of the Armed Forces.[63]

Lord McNally concluded by saying that the issues raised in the debate were substantial and there should be a 'really radical look at voting for our overseas residents and, very importantly, for our military' early in this Parliament.[64]

End Notes

[1] The *Electoral System in Britain Since 1918* by D. Butler, O.U.P, 1963, p 7
[2] ibid, p 8
[3] ibid, p9
[4] ibid, p49
[5] HC Deb 410,c,398 cited in The *Electoral System in Britain Since 1918* by D. Butler, O.U.P, 1963, p 100
[6] As cited by Butler in the work above, p 101
[7] ibid, p101
[8] The *Representation of the People Act 2000*
[9] *Report of the Working Party on Electoral Procedures*, chaired by George Howarth MP, Home Office, 1999
[10] HC Deb 10 January 2005 c13
[11] HC Deb 8 December 2004 cc117-118WH and c120WH
[12] ibid, cc121-122WH
[13] ibid c124WH
[14] Most soldiers will not be able to vote, *Daily Telegraph*, 15 April 2005
[15] *Electoral registration*. First joint report of the Constitutional Affairs and the ODPM: Housing, Planning, Local Government and the Regions Committees 2004-05. HC 243, 2004-05, para 83.
[16] ibid, para 84

[17] Available at http://www.baff.org.uk/baff-factsheets-log-in-first/downloads.htm
[18] ibid, 3.1
[19] ibid, 4.2.2
[20] ibid, 4.4
[21] ibid, Annex A – Consolidated list of recommendations
[22] Voting aid for troops overseas. *Times*, 21 September 2005
[23] HC Deb 25 October 2005 c196
[24] HL Deb 13 February 2006 c1035
[25] HL Deb 13 February 2006 c1035
[26] HL Deb 13 February 2006 c1036
[27] HL Deb 16 March 2006 cGC559
[28] HL Deb 15 May 2006 c30
[29] HL Deb 15 May 2006 c33
[30] HL Deb 7 June 2006 c1276
[31] HL Deb 7 June 2006 c1279
[32] HC Deb 13 June 2006 c711
[33] HC Deb 13 June 2006 c718

[34] HC Deb 13 June 2006 c718

[35] First Standing Committee on Delegated Legislation, 6 Nov 2006

[36] Briefing on Regulations applying measures in the Electoral Administration Act 2006, Electoral Commission, 2006

[37] HL Deb 13 May 2009 c441GC

[38] HL Deb 17 June 2009 c1146

[39] http://www.electoralcommission.org.uk/data/assets/pdf_file/0017/83051/Electoral-Commission-response- to-the-Ministry-of-Justice-FINAL.pdf

[40] The Order and Explanatory Memorandum are available at http://www.opsi.gov.uk/si/si2010/draft/ukdsi_9780111491560_en_1http://www.opsi.gov.uk/si/si2010/draft/em/ukdsiem_9780111491560_en.pdf

[41] http://www.publications.parliament.uk/pa/cm200910/cmgeneral/deleg12/100302/100302s01.htm

[42] http://www.publications.parliament.uk/pa/ld200910/ldhansrd/text/100308-gc0005.htm

[43] http://www.electoralcommission.org.uk/data/assets/electoral_commission_pdf_file/0004/87637/EC09- Service-voter-declaration-extension.pdf

[44] HC Deb 27 June 2007 c30WS

[45] HC Deb 30 October 2008 c1227W and HC Deb 7 July 2008 c1159W

[46] HC Deb 20 July 2009 c1069w

[47] http://www.electoralcommission.org.uk/news-and-media/public-awareness-campaigns/service-voters

[48] http://www.electoralcommission.org.uk/news-and-media/news-releases-old/electoral-commission-media- centre/news-releases-campaigns/service-personnel-encouraged-to-get-ready-for-the-general-election

[49] http://www.electoralcommission.org.uk/data/assets/electoral_commission_pdf_file/0005/79781/EC17---Registering-Service-Voters.pdf

[50] HL Deb 10 November 2009 c137WA

[51] HL Deb 9 December 2009 c1079

[52] http://www.timesonline.co.uk/tol/news/politics/article7069942.ece

[53] HL Deb 6 April 2010 c 1360-62

[54] http://www.electoralcommission.org.uk/ data/assets/pdf_file/0010/93475/EC15.pdf

[55] Report on the administration of the 2010 UK general election, Electoral Commission, July 2010, p 51

[56] HC Deb 18 May 2011 c235W

[57] HC Deb 7 June 2011 c4W

[58] HL Deb 2 March 2011 c1119

[59] HL Deb 2 March 2011 c1127

[60] HL Deb 2 March 2011 c1131

[61] HL Deb 2 March 2011 c1130

[62] HL Deb 2 March 2011 c1131

[63] HL Deb 2 March 2011 c1133

[64] HL Deb 2 March 2011 c1133

In: A History of Voting Rights …
Editor: Nicole P. Springer

ISBN: 978-1-62948-870-7
© 2014 Nova Science Publishers, Inc.

Chapter 4

PRISONERS' VOTING RIGHTS – IN BRIEF*

Isobel White

1. BACKGROUND

Prisoners serving a custodial sentence do not have the right to vote. This ban was set out in Section 3 of the *Representation of the People Act 1983* as amended. Prisoners on remand are able to vote under the provisions of the *Representation of the People Act 2000*.

> The disenfranchisement of prisoners in Great Britain dates back to the *Forfeiture Act 1870* and was linked to the notion of 'civic death'. The 1870 Act denied offenders their rights of citizenship and provided that any person convicted of treason or a felony and sentenced to a term of imprisonment exceeding 12 months lost the right to vote at parliamentary or municipal (local) elections until they had served their sentence. The *Representation of the People Act 1969* introduced a specific provision that convicted persons were legally incapable of voting during the time that they were detained in a penal institution after the *Criminal Law Act 1967* amended the 1870 Act.

---

* This is an edited, reformatted and augmented version of the House of Commons Library (United Kingdom) Standard Note SN06480. The paper contains Parliamentary information licensed under the Open Parliament Licence v1.0., dated October 16, 2013.

The RPA 1969 enacted the recommendations of the Speaker's Conference of 1967-68, one of which was that 'a convicted prisoner who is in custody should not be entitled to vote.' These provisions were later consolidated in the *Representation of the People Act 1983*.

The recommendations put forward in 1999 by the Howarth *Working Party on Electoral Procedures* to allow remand prisoners to be registered to vote were implemented by the *Representation of the People Act 2000*.

Successive governments have held the view that prisoners convicted of serious crimes which have warranted imprisonment have lost the moral authority to vote. On 24 October 2012 the Prime Minister, David Cameron, reiterated his view that

> I do not want prisoners to have the vote, and they should not get the vote—I am very clear about that. If it helps to have another vote in Parliament on another resolution to make it absolutely clear and help put the legal position beyond doubt, I am happy to do that. But no one should be in any doubt: prisoners are not getting the vote under this Government.[1]

The Prison Reform Trust has long campaigned for prisoners to be given the vote; in 2004 the Trust and Unlock (the National Association of Ex-Offenders) launched the 'Barred from Voting' campaign to secure the right to vote for prisoners.

1.1. Prisoners' Voting Rights in Other Countries

Denmark, Finland, Ireland, Spain, Sweden, Cyprus and Switzerland have no ban. In other European countries, electoral disqualification depends on the crime committed, or the length of the sentence; in some countries prisoners are only allowed to vote at certain elections.

Bulgaria, Estonia, Georgia, Hungary and Liechtenstein do not allow prisoners the right to vote.[2]

Russia and Japan exclude all convicted prisoners from voting. In Australia, prisoners can vote in two of seven states, while in the United States, some prisoners are banned from voting even after their release from jail.

2. HIRST V THE UNITED KINGDOM

On 30 March 2004 the European Court of Human Rights (ECtHR) gave its judgement in the case of *Hirst v The United Kingdom*. John Hirst, a prisoner serving a life sentence for manslaughter at Rye Hill Prison in Warwickshire, had challenged the ban on prisoners' voting. Seven judges at the ECtHR ruled that the UK's ban on prisoners' voting breached Article 3 of Protocol 1 of the European Convention on Human Rights, which guarantees 'free elections…under conditions which will ensure the free expression of the opinion of the people in the choice of the legislature.'[3]

The Department of Constitutional Affairs released a statement stating that: 'we have always argued that prisoners should lose the right to vote while in detention because if you commit a crime that is serious, you should lose the right to have a say in how you are governed…This judgement questions that position.'[4]

The Government subsequently appealed the decision. The appeal was held on 27 April 2005 but the final decision was not announced until 6 October 2005. The Grand Chamber of the European Court of Human Rights held, by a majority of 12 to 5, that there had been a violation of Article 3 of Protocol No 1.[5]

3. OTHER ECtHR JUDGEMENTS

FRODL V AUSTRIA

The applicant, who was convicted of murder and sentenced to life imprisonment in 1993 in Austria, alleged that his disenfranchisement, because he was serving a term of imprisonment of more than one year, constituted a breach of his rights under Article 3 of Protocol No 1. The judgement of the European Court of Human Rights, which became final on 4 October 2010, was that there had been a breach of Article 3 of Protocol No 1.

SCOPPOLA V ITALY (NO 3)

The applicant, Franco Scoppola was sentenced in 2002 by the Assize Court to life imprisonment for murder, attempted murder, ill-treatment of members of his family and unauthorised possession of a firearm. Under Italian law his life sentence entailed a lifetime ban from public office, amounting to permanent forfeiture of his right to vote. Appeals by the applicant against the ban were unsuccessful. Scoppola subsequently complained that the ban on public office imposed as a result of his life sentence had amounted to a permanent forfeiture of his entitlement to vote. The Court's judgement in January 2011 was that there had been a breach of Article 3 of Protocol No.1.

GREENS AND MT

Robert Greens and M.T. were both serving a prison sentence at HM Prison Peterhead at the time their applications were lodged with the European Court in 2008. The two prisoners had sought to be registered as voters but their applications were refused by the Electoral Registration Officer. Greens and M.T. complained that the refusal to enroll them on the electoral register for domestic and European elections was in violation of Article 3 of Protocol No. 1. The European Court's judgement on 23 November 2010 was that there had been a violation of Article 3 for both applicants.

4. THE LABOUR GOVERNMENT'S CONSULTATION PAPERS

The first consultation document on the voting rights of prisoners issued by the Labour Government was published on 14 December 2006:

> The paper sets out the background to the case of Hirst v UK, the conclusions reached by the Grand Chamber, and proposes a number of potential options on which the Government would welcome views. This is a contentious issue. The Government are firm in their belief that individuals who have committed an offence serious enough to warrant a term of imprisonment, should not be able to vote while in prison. None the less, we recognise that we must decide how to respond to the Grand Chamber's judgment.[6]

The document set out the possible options for the enfranchisement of prisoners and sought views on the retention of the ban on voting for all convicted, detained prisoners. The options included relating disenfranchisement to the length of sentence and allowing judges to determine whether the right to vote should be withdrawn from an offender.[7]

The second stage consultation paper was published on 8 April 2009; the paper set out four options as to how the enfranchisement of convicted prisoners determined by their sentence could be implemented.[8]

4.1. Reports of the Joint Committee on Human Rights

The House of Lords and House of Commons Joint Committee on Human Rights considered the ECtHR judgment in its sixteenth report of 2006-07 and noted that:

> The continued failure to remove the blanket ban, enfranchising at least part of the prison population, is clearly unlawful. It is also a matter for regret that the Government should seek views on retaining the current blanket ban, thereby raising expectations that this could be achieved, when in fact, this is the one option explicitly ruled out by the European Court.
>
> 79. We recommend that the Government bring forward a solution as soon as possible, preferably in the form of an urgent Remedial Order. We strongly recommend that the Government publish a draft Remedial Order as part of its second stage of consultation. We would be disappointed if a legislative solution were not in force in adequate time to allow the necessary preparations to be made for the next general election.[9]

The Joint Committee again noted the Government's delay in responding to the ECtHR judgment in its 31st report of 2007-08.[10] The Committee once again recommended action to resolve the issue and reiterated this in its fourth report of 2008-09.

4.2. Resolution of the Council of Europe's Committee of Ministers

On 3 December 2009 the Council of Europe's Committee of Ministers also called on the UK Government to lift the blanket ban on prisoners' voting.

At their meeting on 2 - 4 March 2010 the Committee of Ministers issued a warning to the UK Government to "rapidly adopt" measures to enable prisoners to vote in the forthcoming general election; at their meeting on 1-3 June 2010 the Committee of Ministers expressed 'profound regret' that the ban had not been lifted and in December 2010 called upon the UK authorities to present an action plan for implementation of the judgment which includes a clear timetable for the adoption of the measures envisaged.

5. THE COALITION GOVERNMENT'S PROPOSALS FOR ACTION

At Prime Minister's Questions on 3 November 2010, David Cameron was asked about prisoners' voting rights:

> **Gareth Johnson (Dartford) (Con):** Does the Prime Minister agree that it would be wrong for convicted prisoners to be able to vote, as suggested by the European Court of Human Rights? The incarceration of convicted prisoners should mean a loss of rights for that individual, and that must surely include the right to vote.
>
> **The Prime Minister:** I completely agree with my hon. Friend. It makes me physically ill even to contemplate having to give the vote to anyone who is in prison. Frankly, when people commit a crime and go to prison, they should lose their rights, including the right to vote. But we are in a situation that I am afraid we have to deal with. This is potentially costing us £160 million, so we have to come forward with proposals, because I do not want us to spend that money; it is not right. So, painful as it is, we have to sort out yet another problem that was just left to us by the last Government.[11]

5.1. Compensation

Mark Harper, then Parliamentary Secretary, Cabinet Office, said on 2 November 2010 that there were more than 1,000 cases of prisoners seeking compensation because the UK had not complied with the European Court's ruling and that there was 'a real risk that judges will award millions of pounds in damages to be paid by our taxpayers to prisoners who have been denied the vote.'[12]

On 18 February 2011 the High Court ruled that compensation claims from prisoners who were unable to vote in the 2010 general election would not succeed. The Court was told that claims had been launched in county courts nationwide by 585 serving prisoners, with a further 1,000 potential cases pending. Mr Justice Langstaff said

> I hold that there are no reasonable grounds in domestic law for bringing a claim for damages or a declaration for being disenfranchised whilst a prisoner. Statute precludes it. Case law is against it. European authority is against the payment of compensatory damages in respect of it. A claim for a declaration is not hopeless, but difficult.[13]

5.2. Statement on Prisoners' Voting Rights 20 December 2010

On 20 December 2010, the Government announced that offenders sentenced to a custodial sentence of less than four years would have the right to vote in UK Westminster Parliamentary and European Parliament elections, unless the judge considered this inappropriate when making the sentence. The Government noted that there were 'in the region of 2,500 claims [for compensation] before the European Court of Human Rights which have been suspended pending implementation' and added:

> Governments have an absolute duty to uphold the rule of law. And at this of all times we must avoid risking taxpayers' money in ways that the public would rightly condemn. In the light of this, and of the legacy left by the last Government, the only responsible course is to implement the judgment, and to do so in a way which ensures the most serious offenders continue to lose the right to vote.[14]

No timetable was announced for the proposed legislation.

6. DEBATE IN PARLIAMENT

6.1. Westminster Hall Debate 11 January 2011

Philip Hollobone (Conservative) secured a Westminster Hall debate on prisoners' voting rights on 11 January 2011.[15] Mr Hollobone argued that the ban on convicted prisoners being able to vote should be retained and that the Government should not comply with the European Court's ruling.

Chris Bryant, speaking for the Opposition, also supported the retention of the ban although he said that he disagreed with those Members who had suggested that the UK should leave the European Court of Human Rights.[16] Two Members spoke in favour of removing the blanket ban. Kate Green (Labour) believed it was morally right that prisoners should have the opportunity to vote[17] and Sir Peter Bottomley (Conservative) also supported giving prisoners the vote and spoke about the rehabilitation of prisoners.[18]

6.2. Political and Constitutional Reform Committee's Inquiry

The Political and Constitutional Reform Committee took evidence from Lord Mackay of Clashfern, Aidan O'Neill QC and Dr Eric Metcalfe of JUSTICE on 1 February 2011.[19] The Committee's inquiry was intended to inform the backbench debate on prisoners' voting rights due to be held in the House of Commons on Thursday 10 February 2011.

The Committee published its report on 8 February 2011 and concluded:

> 22. **The House is being asked to decide whether it both "acknowledges the treaty obligations of the UK" and "supports the current situation in which no prisoner is able to vote except those imprisoned for contempt, default or on remand".** The evidence we have received from our witnesses, including a former Lord Chancellor, is that, however morally justifiable it might be, this current situation is illegal under international law founded on the UK's treaty obligations.[20]

6.3. Backbench Debate on 10 February 2011

The motion, which was not binding on the Government, was in the names of David Davis, Jack Straw, Dominic Raab, Stephen Phillips, Philip Hollobone and John Baron:

> That this House notes the ruling of the European Court of Human Rights in Hirst v the United Kingdom in which it held that there had been no substantive debate by members of the legislature on the continued justification for maintaining a general restriction on the right of prisoners to vote; acknowledges the treaty obligations of the UK; is of the opinion

that legislative decisions of this nature should be a matter for democratically-elected lawmakers; and supports the current situation in which no sentenced prisoner is able to vote except those imprisoned for contempt, default or on remand.[21]

The majority of Members who spoke in the debate supported the motion. Dominic Grieve, the Attorney General, described the dilemma faced by the Government: 'how can we find a way to persuade the Court to respect the views that the legislature may express without having to withdraw from the Convention or the Council of Europe entirely, which...would not come without cost or consequence for this country.'[22]

The motion was agreed on division by 234 to 22.

7. THE ECtHR DEADLINE FOR THE UK TO INTRODUCE LEGISLATION

On 1 March 2011 the Government announced that it had referred the *Greens and MT* judgement to the Grand Chamber of the European Court of Human Rights, in effect appealing the Court's decision. On 11 April 2011 the Grand Chamber rejected the Government's request for an appeal hearing and the six month deadline for the UK government to introduce legislative proposals to remove the blanket ban on all serving prisoners from voting was triggered on 11 April 2011 when the Court's judgment of 23 November 2010 became final.

7.1. Extension of the ECHR Six Month Deadline

On 6 September 2011 the Government announced that the ECtHR had agreed to an extension of the six month deadline. The extension to the deadline had been requested to take account of the referral of *Scoppola v Italy (No 3)* (a case similar to that of *Greens and MT*) to the Grand Chamber which would not be heard until 2 November 2011.

The Grand Chamber's judgment in the case of *Scoppola v Italy (No 3)* was announced on 22 May 2012. The Court found that there had been no violation of Article 3 of Protocol No. 1 (right to free elections) to the European Convention on Human Rights and that Franco Scoppola's disenfranchisement was not disproportionate.

The Court confirmed the judgment in the case of *Hirst (no 2) v the United Kingdom* but accepted the UK Government's argument that member States should have a wide discretion as to how they regulate a ban on prisoners voting 'both as regards the types of offence that should result in the loss of the vote and as to whether disenfranchisement should be ordered by a judge in an individual case or should result from general application of a law'.[23]

The delivery of the judgement in the case of *Scoppola v Italy (No 3)* meant that the UK Government had six months from the date of the judgment, 22 May 2012, to bring forward legislative proposals to amend the law on prisoners' voting rights.

8. RECENT DEVELOPMENTS

The Attorney General, Dominic Grieve, appeared before the Justice Committee on 24 October 2012 and was asked about the *Scoppola* judgment. Mr Grieve said that

> the issue is whether the United Kingdom wishes to be in breach of its international obligations and what that does reputationally for the UK. As I have stressed, ultimately this is not a matter where there is not parliamentary sovereignty; there plainly is. Parliament gives and can take away; Governments can leave the Council of Europe if they choose to do so. All I am saying is that it is quite clear, and is accepted by the Government, that in so far as the Scopola judgment is concerned it imposes an international legal obligation on us.[24]

8.1. Letter to the *Times* on 2 November 2012

On 2 November 2012 the *Times* published a letter about prisoners' voting rights from eleven legal academics and judges, including the former Conservative Lord Chancellor, Lord Mackay of Clashfern, and the former Lord Chief Justice, Lord Woolf of Barnes. The authors of the letter suggested that

> Disregard for the European Convention would encourage those nations whose commitment to the rule of law is tenuous. It also contravenes the Ministerial Code. Moreover, such defiance of the Court would not be on a par with measures such as the "veto" of the EU

financial treaty, the proposed opt-out from EU criminal measures, or the threat to veto the EU budget. All those measures, whatever their merits, are perfectly lawful. In this case the Prime Minister appears set upon a course which is clearly unlawful.[25]

9. GEORGE MCGEOCH AND PETER CHESTER CASES

A legal challenge to the ban was made in 2010 by George McGeoch, who is serving a life sentence in Dumfries for murder. McGeoch tried to have his name added to the electoral register but was unsuccessful. His lawyers argued that his rights as an EU citizen were being denied because he will not be able to vote in the European Parliamentary elections.[26]

Peter Chester, also serving a life sentence for murder, brought a case challenging the blanket ban on voting by prisoners.

Appeals by both McGeoch and Chester were heard by the Supreme Court in June 2013. The Court considered whether McGeoch could claim a right under EU law to vote in local elections and European Parliamentary elections and, in the case of Peter Chester, the Court considered whether the ban on voting in UK Parliamentary and European Parliamentary elections was incompatible with Article 3 of Protocol 1 of the ECHR and/or whether the blanket ban was incompatible with EU law.[27]

The Supreme Court gave its judgment on 16 October 2013 and unanimously dismissed both appeals.[28] The Court ruled that 'with regard to EU law, this does not provide an individual right to vote paralleling that recognised by the ECtHR in its case-law'.

10. PUBLICATION OF A DRAFT BILL ON 22 NOVEMBER 2012

On 22 November 2012 the Lord Chancellor, Chris Grayling, made a statement to the House of Commons and announced the publication of a draft Bill, the *Voting Eligibility (Prisoners) Draft Bill* for pre-legislative scrutiny which sets out three options:

- A ban for prisoners sentenced to 4 years or more.
- A ban for prisoners sentenced to more than 6 months.
- A ban for all convicted prisoners – a restatement of the existing ban.[29]

11. JOINT SELECT COMMITTEE

On publication of the draft Bill the Lord Chancellor also announced that the Leaders of both Houses had written to the Liaison Committees to propose that a joint Select Committee should be established to conduct pre-legislative scrutiny of the draft Bill.[30]

The House of Lords started the process of establishing a joint Select Committee in January and sent a message to the Commons.[31] A motion in the House of Commons to agree with the message from the House of Lords and to nominate the Members of the House of Commons to serve on the Committee, was agreed on 16 April 2013.[32]

The members of the Joint Select Committee from the House of Commons are:

Crispin Blunt (Conservative)
Steve Brine (Conservative)
Lorely Burt (Liberal Democrat)
Nick Gibb (Conservative)
Sir Alan Meale (Labour)
Derek Twigg (Labour)

On 14 May 2013 the House of Lords agreed a motion to appoint six members to the joint committee.[33] The members are:

Lord Dholakia (Liberal Democrat)
Baroness Gibson of Market Rasen (Labour)
Baroness Noakes (Conservative)
Lord Norton of Louth (Conservative)
Lord Peston (Labour)
Lord Phillips of Worth Matravers (Non-affiliated)

The motion also stated that the Joint Select Committee was to report on the draft Bill by 31 October 2013. Subsequent motions in both Houses on 10 October 2013 changed this date to 18 December 2013.[34]

The Joint Select Committee held its first evidence session on 19 June 2013. The Committee's web pages give details of the evidence sessions.[35]

27,498 prisoners aged over 18 are serving sentences of under 4 years as at 30 September 2012. A proportion of these will not be eligible to vote because they are foreign nationals.

End Notes

[1] HC Deb 24 October 2012 c923

[2] For further information about the current position in the Council of Europe countries see Dep 2012-1305

[3] The Judgment is on the ECHR's website

[4] http://news.bbc.co.uk/1/hi/england/coventry_warwickshire/3583855.stm

[5] http://hudoc.echr.coe.int/sites/eng-press/pages/search.aspx?i=001-70442

[6] HL Deb 14 December 2006 cWS203

[7] *Voting rights of convicted prisoners detained within the United Kingdom- the UK Government's response to the Grand Chamber of the European Court of Human Rights judgment in the case of Hirst v. the United Kingdom: consultation paper.* Department for Constitutional Affairs, 14 December 2006

[8] *Voting rights of convicted prisoners detained within the United Kingdom: second stage consultation.* Consultation Paper CP6/09, Ministry of Justice, 8 April 2009

[9] *Monitoring the Government's response to court judgments finding breaches of human rights.* Sixteenth report of the House of Commons and House of Lords Joint Committee on Human Rights. HC 728, 2006-07

[10] *Monitoring the Government's response to human rights judgments: annual report 2008.* Thirty-first report of the House of Commons and House of Lords Joint Committee on Human Rights. HC 1078, 2007-08

[11] HC Deb 3 November 2010 c921

[12] HC Deb 2 November 2010 c772

[13] *Tovey and Another v Ministry of Justice* [2011] EWHC 271 (QB) Prisoners lose voting compensation bid, *Independent,*18 February 2011

[14] HC Deb 20 December 2010 c151WS

[15] HC Deb 11 January 2011 c1WH

[16] HC Deb 11 January 2011 c20WH

[17] HC Deb 11 January 2011 c7WH and c8WH

[18] HC Deb 11 January 2011 c16WH

[19] *Voting by convicted prisoners,* Political and Constitutional Reform Committee fifth report 2010-12, minutes of evidence, HC 776

[20] *ibid*

[21] http://www.publications.parliament.uk/pa/cm/cmfbusi/a01.htm

[22] HC Deb 10 February 2011 c512

[23] *Court says that it is up to member States to decide how to regulate the ban on prisoners voting,* European Court of Human rights press release, 22 May 2012

[24] The work of the Attorney General, oral evidence to the Justice Committee, 24 October 2012

[25] Votes for prisoners, letter to the *Times,* 2 November 2012

[26] UK dithering over prisoners' voting rights, *Guardian,* 15 July 2012

[27] For further details see the Supreme Court website: McGeoch case and Chester case

[28] Supreme Court press release, 16 October 2013

[29] The *Voting Eligibility (Prisoners) Draft Bill,* Cm 8499, November 2012

[30] HC Deb 22 November 2012 c746

[31] HL Deb 15 January 2013 c596

[32] HC Deb 16 April 2013 c294

[33] HL Deb 14 May 2013 c271

[34] HL Deb 10 October 2013 c182 and HC Deb 9 October 2013 c269

[35] Draft Voting Eligibility (Prisoners) Bill Joint Select Committee

INDEX

D

E

F